Missions for Thoughtful Gamers

Copyright by

Andrew Cutting
&
ETC Press
2011

ISBN: 978-1-257-97970-7
Library of Congress Control Number: 2011936489

TEXT: The text of this work is licensed under a Creative Commons Attribution-NonCommercial-NonDerivative 2.5 License (http://creativecommons.org/licenses/by-nc-nd/2.5/)

IMAGES: All images appearing in this work are used and reproduced with the permission of the respective copyright owners, and are not released into the Creative Commons. The respective owners reserve all rights.

Illustrations by the author
Design, composition, & Cover Art by Ethan Gladding

Acknowledgments

This book would never have happened without the opportunity to teach Game Studies at London Metropolitan University. I have learnt a lot from the students there. Vanda Corrigan prompted me to begin my own journey into contemporary gaming and has been a genial guide and companion along the way. Anne Karpf encouraged me to clarify and pursue the book's main project. The brevity of the Further Reading section disguises the debt I owe to the many people, from bloggers to professors, who have written eloquently about games. Thanks to Drew Davidson and Ethan Gladding at ETC Press for helping bring the book into form, and to my partner, Terry, for many years of love and support.

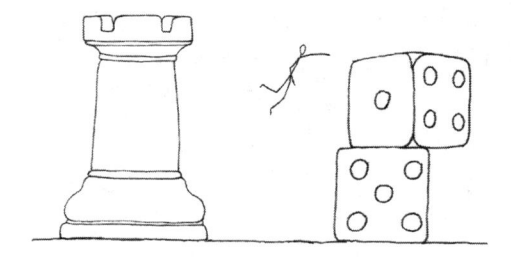

Table of Contents

1   DEMO / The Gamer's Oath

9   Let this one room be your game-world

13   TUTORIAL / Playthinking: how to use this book

20   Make some rules
24   Think systematically
28   Perform as a human Tic-Tac-Toe machine

33   EPISODE 1: HIDDEN LANDS / Videogames as enquiry

39   Turn your life-story into an autobiogame
42   Engame the gamer
45   Re-center a game's cultural perspective
48   Try Surrealism
51   Auralize an audiogame
55   Spot stories that want to be games
58   Conceive a Holocaust, civilian, or pacifist war game

63   BOSS FIGHT / Exploring 'violence'

70   Fondle your weapon
73   Defeat your symbolic father
76   Query biceps and breasts
79   Trace the Hero's Journey
83   Relive your greatest victory or defeat
85   Contemplate your in-game deaths
88   Play to lose
91   Feel the blows

95 EPISODE 2: THE INNERMOST CAVE/ Gnōthi sauton

102 Know your pleasure principle
105 Keep a gamer's diary
109 Unpick the hook and bathe in the after-glow
113 Invite a character home
117 Become cyborg
120 Practice the inner game
123 Observe your body playing
126 Greet your boredom
129 Measure your playing habits
132 Salivate, savor, digest

137 SIDE-QUESTS AND MINI-GAMES / Scholarly gaming

141 Purify the language of the gamer tribe
144 Deconstruct game hype
148 Pretend you're visiting from Mars
150 Report from the arcade
154 Enter the world of stick-people
157 Analogize a digital game
160 Co-play a single-player game
163 Go gray

167 EPILOGUE / Gaming's highest ideals

173 Monitor gamers in the media
175 Name that learning
178 Remember the electronic graveyard

181 End cut-scene

186 Credits: Further reading

DEMO

The Gamer's Oath

No Playing Here. Apparently some things in life are too serious to be treated as a game. At funeral services, parents forbid children their toys. In courtrooms, the judge will fine any jury-member found playing puzzles on a mobile phone. Legendary is the anger of lovers who discover they were seduced for a bet. Most of us shudder to imagine what kind of 'games' would thrill stalkers, pedophiles, and torturers. We don't expect theater-nurses to score points against each other while assisting at open-heart surgery.

The Sworn Gamer, committed to treating all life as primarily or nothing but a game, therefore makes an ethical choice.

Avid gamers, among whom you might count yourself, sacrifice some breadth of view, capability, and social association for narrowness of expertise. Utter specialists, whether in the field of videogames, medieval church music, or quantum physics, impress few people apart from each other and risk failure of ordinary human connection. But the heroic individual determined to carry the gaming attitude into every corner of life – as rakes, rascals, and revolutionaries have done in previous centuries – risks not merely social isolation but legal sanction and psychological disintegration.

Can you treat life as a game when faced by personal and national crises such as imprisonment, bereavement, terminal illness, catastrophic natural disaster, or civil war? Gamers living in the comfort of industrially developed, economically wealthy, politically liberal countries are privileged individuals who rarely face circumstances that detain them for very long from their preferred form of entertainment. People have risked their life for a book, faced death more bravely because of a song, and taken up arms over a statue. Would you swear to make gaming your rock amid life's turmoil and the last thing you'd ever surrender?

Videogames inspire passions that crystallize a life-attitude not unique to the current era. Just because they're so popular and seemingly modern today does not at all guarantee them a privileged future. Like everything else within human culture, in order to survive they must prove their ongoing fitness and adaptability in serving our needs. Historically they're as yet barely a blip. It's quite possible they'll turn out, with hindsight, to be a dead-end: a distraction from what play can be in its ongoing importance for our species.

We can be confident that humans will always play games of some sort. As man is a storytelling animal, so is he also a creature that plays. *Homo ludens* is Dutch historian Johan Huizinga's phrase from the 1930s. Play is fundamental to human development, most obviously in childhood, and in every stage of life playfulness is part of feeling alive. True, many of the conditions of modern life, such as requirements to present a serious, professional attitude in the workplace, discourage adults from being playful. All this does, however, is displace the in-built urge to play into other spheres of life, most obviously leisure time. This may take the form of unstructured playfulness, expressed for example in water-cooler humor, or more organized games, such as the various kinds of videogame, that provide an alternative world whose rules are mercifully less complicated than real life.

Wanting to be a full-time play-boy or play-girl is one thing, committing to the idea that every aspect of human experience is fundamentally playable is another.

Consider Pascal's Wager, arguably the first expression of what's now called game theory (mathematical analysis of probability and decision-making applied to economic and social behavior). Proposed in the 1600s by a French philosopher, the Wager begins with an ultimatum.

God either exists or He doesn't. 'A game is being played… you must wager.' How should you decide whether or not to believe in God when, on a purely rational basis, you cannot know whether He exists or not? Well, if He doesn't, you won't lose anything whether you believe in Him or not. But if He does, you've an eternal heaven to gain by believing in Him. Therefore you should wager that He exists.

Needless to say, this argument hasn't convinced everyone. A simpler, less theological example of a thoroughgoing gaming attitude to life appears in Luke Rhinehart's novel, *The Dice Man*. When a frustrated psychiatrist decides to start living by the throw of the dice, creative mayhem ensues.

Or we might look back to duelists and gladiators, who literally played games of life and death, though not always out of choice. Today's gamers patently would *not* risk their life for real in the way they repeatedly do within the fictional worlds shown onscreen. Instead, by digitally simulating diverse environments with apparently ever-increasing realism, videogames enable us to play the life-risking hero safely, hypothetically. They allow us to experiment imaginatively with what a gaming attitude might be like if carried into every area of life.

This experiment has already moved outside the confines of bedrooms and living rooms in various ways. Perhaps most obviously, wireless networking brings closer the prospect of online multiplayer gaming potentially occurring everywhere and all the time: ubiquitously, pervasively. Players might be spread across steamy rainforests, sun-drenched beaches, snowy mountainsides, busy shopping malls, school playgrounds, fast-food restaurants, motorway service stations, doctors' waiting rooms, motel bedrooms, and anywhere else you can think of, at any time of the day or night. Friend races friend on either side of the globe while stranger duels stranger sitting three stools away down the bar.

Alternate reality games, by contrast, abandon conventional videogame equipment and use information posted to World Wide Web sites and other platforms to lead players on a mystery adventure in real time and space. Crucially, ARGs are a form of storytelling that aims to perfect the illusion that their fictional world is real, often on the lines of a conspiracy, for example by casting the players as themselves, not fictional characters, and by sending players hoax emails and text messages.

In addition to ARGs, there are many related forms of playful participation occurring in our streets, parks, and other public spaces, such as live-action role-playing (LARPing), mobile-phone treasure hunts, geocaching, 'happenings,' parkour, and flash mobs.

Numerous reality television shows, meanwhile, most famously *Big Brother*, provide further evidence of a widespread desire to live, at least for a period, inside an encompassing game-world.

For the cautious and the skeptical, the idea that all of life is playable can be true only for the space of a weekend or only as metaphor. All the world's a stage, happy families sing in harmony, life's a football match, and some lucky people are dealt a winning hand at birth. Such clichés help us to make sense of our existence. They're a means of understanding and sometimes of misunderstanding.

On the other hand, it's also become intellectually fashionable to claim that many areas of life have literally become games. Career progression, electioneering, international diplomacy, high-tech warfare, and stock-market trading are obvious examples of supposedly serious domains that have become increasingly unreal and game-like. Personal life is also affected, as illustrated by the so-called dating game and the materialistic social competition known as keeping up with the Joneses.

For an explanation of this phenomenon, take your pick from various theories about our (post)modern condition. One observes that our experience of the world is now highly mediated by computer and television screens, so that physical reality is displaced by images, signs, simulations, and the virtual. Another blames bureaucrats and experts who seek to regulate and manage every conceivable area of life using more-or-less abstract models divorced from the actual experience of front-line workers and ordinary people. Or consider the apparent collapse (along with the Berlin Wall in 1989) of any ideological alternative to free-market capitalism and the general fading of political class-consciousness, which together seem to leave myriad individuals each chasing advertisers' dreams of celebrity lifestyles awarded with dubious justice to those smart or lucky enough to win at the game of fame and fortune.

Videogames already simulate many areas of life. Despite this apparent variety, however, *how* life is playable onscreen depends on what game developers have so far devised. The extent of their thinking is indicated by the existing range of game genres and hybrids. For educationalists and political activists who seriously believe that play – and perhaps *only* play – is capable of generating solutions to the world's most intractable problems, games must move beyond their predominant function as commercial entertainment and become more diverse, more subversive, more genuinely creative, and thus more democratic, all while staying enjoyable. (Several excellent books develop these arguments: see the first paragraph of the Further Reading section.)

Looking back to games of the past, we find that all play appears to be of certain fundamental kinds, such as competitions and sessions of make-believe. In every historical period, humans have developed amusements based on similar patterns of physical, intellectual, and artistic activity. Thus people will presumably enjoy racing, verbal sparring, and dressing up, in some manner or other, till the end of time. Certainly they feature in plenty of science fiction movies set in the future.

It's not this underlying basis of play, but the particular forms taken by videogames as we hitherto know them that limit how gamers might currently imagine life as playable.

The percussionist views every object as a potential instrument. The painter never goes without his sketchbook. The free-runner constantly surveys her environment for possible routes. So the Sworn Gamer must keep a daily lookout for opportunities to play.

Moment-by-moment responsiveness to life is a general precondition of creativity in any art-form. Assuming that all of life is potentially playable, progressive game designers, critics, and educators will adopt a permanent stance of readiness. Game concepts wait to be found not just in currently taboo or unfashionable topics but also in the undiscovered here and now of any and every place, any and every time, any and everyone's experience.

When rave reviews imply that videogames can provide peak life experiences, maybe this is mere rhetorical exaggeration. Are you one of those willing to take play more seriously: to recognize it as a fundamental source of meaning for you, as important as things like health and friendship, or creativity and faith, without which it would scarcely be meaningful for you to be in the world at all? As a thoughtful gamer, your overarching mission in this book is to bridge the apparent gulf between everyday enjoyment of gaming, so often explained away under the catch-all label of 'fun,' and big philosophical questions such as Who am I? What is it like to be me in this world? What is real? What is true? What makes a good life? These questions may sound pretentious to ask about gaming, but ultimately nothing less will do, and one day you may well answer some of them before breakfast.

Your journey to discover answers – let's call it the Gamer's Journey – will not be a merely intellectual one, but also a moral, spiritual, and of course playful one. Some might say such a quest for meaning is unending, and that we should never foreclose our future potential by believing we've arrived at definitive answers. On the other hand, a life in which *no* promises, vows, or dedications are ever made, *no* ceremonies, conferments, or other formal rituals are ever gone through, is, at least in part, a deferred life. Such things help make us, and without them we miss ways to become and to understand who we are.

Here's one possible wording of a Gamer's Oath: 'I seek to play here, now, everywhere, and always. Accepting that playfulness is for me an essential part of a sane response to human existence, I recognize the sacred duty of expressing and evolving the spirit of gaming.' Ideally you'll discover your own wording, as authentic, unpretentious, and needful to you as a heartfelt poem. It'll be a more substantial statement of commitment than the mere wish, given the chance, to play videogames as often as you like for the rest of your life.

Embark then, if you dare, upon the Gamer's Journey that will bring you to a fuller understanding, through a series of missions, of what your Oath might be. Attempt every mission and your journey will be epic; this book is deceptively slim.

Let this one room be your game-world

Here is your first mission. Wherever you are at this moment, as you read these words, look around. The space surrounding you may be large or small, indoors or out, public or private, empty or full, familiar or strange. What possibilities of gameplay can you imagine occurring in *this* place: here and now and with no beyond?

Many videogames take the player on a journey through space, often to explore and conquer it. However, the carefully rendered game-world – celebrated in marketing hype as 'vast' – is mostly inert backdrop. Even games which claim you can interact with everything in your environment are limited by what the designers have actually programmed. For most of the time the player character might as well be wearing boxing gloves. Not this time: what could a player character do where you are right now by taking the gloves off?

One familiar version of this exercise is to magnify your surroundings so that objects appear many times their usual size. The premise of your game might then be how a human being can navigate a world that's suddenly become bizarrely and dangerously out-of-scale – as in the black-and-white classic film, *The Incredible Shrinking Man*, where a spider and other mundane objects become monstrously huge. Or your heroes might be creatures who are already small, like the characters of Disney-Pixar's *Toy Story* series or Marvel Comics' Ant-Man. What aids and powers will enable players to navigate the outsized obstacle course, and what traps and foes await them? What will be the milestones, ultimate goal, and heroic story of their quest?

Alternatively, what magical behaviors can you imagine for the everyday objects around you? Where are the secret portals and warp-holes from other worlds, who or what comes through them, how friendly are these invaders, or how do they need the player's help? What communication devices enable the player to reach beyond the space without actually leaving? What mysterious and puzzling objects are hidden around the room, how did they come to be here, who possessed them previously, and what powers stored within them await to be unlocked?

This is an exercise you can do anywhere, ideally in many different locations. Attend closely enough, and every space is unique… implying the possibility of an endless number of games or game variants. Try it when you're cooped up with strangers – in a waiting room, train carriage, elevator, or airplane, say. Any second now there'll be an accident or disaster and you'll be trapped with these people and left to pass the time while awaiting rescue. Tensions will boil over between the inmates, or the room will become a giant puzzle you must solve from inside in order to unlock the exit (as in so-called escape-the-room games).

Perhaps you'll find inspiration in 'Tango', a short film by the Polish animator Zbigniew Rybczyński, whose central idea has been borrowed by various music videos and television advertisements. The scene is a sparsely-furnished bedroom. When a red ball drops through the open window, a boy in shorts climbs in to fetch it. Various other characters enter, either through the window or one of the two doors. Each character exits and then reenters to repeat exactly the same motion as before. Without bumping into each other, they weave an elegant, choreographed dance. Gradually each character makes his or her final exit. The boy is the last to go, climbing out with his rescued ball for one last time and leaving the room empty once more. Who or what enters the space you currently occupy? Whence do they come, and whither do they go? How might their paths cross, and what might the player do to put them in each other's way or to untangle their knots?

In H.G. Wells's *The Time Machine* a Victorian scientist mounts his machine and travels nowhere in space but thousands of years in time. The space occupied by his London laboratory in the 1890s transforms into a garden reclaimed by nature after the future collapse of civilization, and then into a desolate beach at the very end of the world, beneath a dying sun. Similarly he can travel to the same spot centuries or millennia in the past. Even at different times of day or seasons of the year the immediate space you're occupying at this moment changes its character. Or what temporal paradoxes could arise through the sudden visit of your past or future self?

Your bedroom is an obvious choice of room. For many of us, this is where our inner worlds are most intimately expressed, in our dreams, relationships, illnesses, and personal items. It's the room we know best and which has greatest emotional resonance. Your bed alone is a potentially vast landscape.

To take this exercise to an extreme, imagine games taking place on your body: in the folds and pockets of your clothes, on the surfaces and crevices of your skin and hair.

Once you enter the interior of the body, the potential space expands again. Medicine has revealed wondrous landscapes beneath the skin, from the level of organs down to that of cells, all full of activity and potentially a scene for action. In *Fantastic Voyage* (another outstanding movie memory from my childhood) a group of scientists aboard their submarine are miniaturized and injected into a man's body in order to navigate through his bloodstream, fight off antibodies and saboteurs along the way, and carry out microsurgery on a blood clot in the brain that will otherwise kill him within the hour. There's a game premise here.

Even vaster as potential fields of play are the realms of the conscious and unconscious mind. Consider those individuals confined within the cells of prisons, asylums, and monasteries. Extraordinary worlds of memory, desire, microscopic awareness, and cosmic drama must occupy their voluntary or enforced solitude. Take these incarcerates as your models for how to imagine a game that's all in the mind.

TUTORIAL

Playthinking

The archetypal thinker is a heavy-browed philosopher, too deep in contemplation to notice the toddler and its toys at his feet, nor the garish colors of a videogame flickering on a television screen nearby. By convention, thought is serious and weighty, in contrast to frivolous, lighthearted play. One is for responsible, plodding adults, the other for carefree, skipping children.

Yet we can enjoy thinking while finding play hard work: ask quiz-show contestants and professional musicians. Wherever humans are especially creative, thought and play combine: inventors, performers, artists, researchers, and entrepreneurs of all kinds and at all levels become so immersed in the task to hand that distinctions between work and play, thought and action, effort and pleasure, become irrelevant. Many people, whether famous or obscure, have known this experience, if only on occasions.

The title phrase of this book, 'thoughtful gamers,' could well be an instant turn-off for those players who automatically associate thinking with work, tedium, and futility. Being called thoughtless is nothing compared to how gamers are often described in the media. 'Thoughtful gamer' is not a contradiction in terms, though.

Play already has its specialist thinkers, including psychologists, anthropologists, game designers, and the newly-named ludologists (game theorists, from the Latin *ludus*, meaning game). Players, too, respond creatively and critically to particular games and gaming practices, for example through discussions in online forums, fan art and fiction. The emerging academic discipline that attempts to pull together this diverse field is called Game Studies.

Game here, as throughout this book, refers especially to the wide variety of digital game genres and platforms that have developed during the last thirty-or-so years to the point of eclipsing in popularity more traditional games, such as playground, card, board, and party games. We'll also set aside those games more properly called sports, as well as gambling. These activities, though close cousins, form separate fields from the increasingly mainstream, worldwide entertainment phenomenon now known as gaming.

Even non-gamers know what's happened. Passengers on buses and subway trains while away the journey by arranging rows of explosive jewels, managing a cartoon farm, or controlling a killer shark, all on their mobile telephone. In airport departure lounges, brothers sit side-by-side playing football or racing sports cars on scuffed handheld devices. In seaside and city-center amusement arcades, teenagers joggle on dance mats and strive to knock each other out with high-kicking martial-arts moves. After dinner each evening, neighbors and work colleagues play sword 'n' sorcery epics on laptop computers against people living thousands of miles away and known to each other only by their online nickname. Several times a year, midnight hoards rush to buy the latest installment of a shooting game that for the next two weeks will obsess them night and day via consoles attached to high-definition television screens.

So many different types of game, player, platform, and playing situation, in fact, with more emerging every year, that it's difficult to generalize accurately or without already being out of date. For convenience I'll use the umbrella terms 'games' and 'videogames' even though in reality these encompass a huge variety of very different things. The wider your own experience as a gamer, the more exceptions will occur to you as you read on, as well as alternative examples to the ones given.

This book invites you to become an active, questioning producer of knowledge about games by adopting the role of *playthinker* and undertaking missions in game play, design, analysis, criticism, and research.

> Playthinker, *n.*, a thinker who plays or a player who thinks; someone who plays at thinking, someone who thinks by playing.

Grammatical purists would hyphenate: play-thinker. Signaling a yoking of two separate terms, the hyphen should disappear only when, with popular usage over time, the linguistic fusion into a single concept is complete. By omitting the hyphen, we jump ahead to invoke the personification of an already-achieved evolution… a future being who is yourself in the making.

Starting with three fundamental concepts of game design – rules, systems, and computation – you'll develop your playthinking powers with the help of various game-related exercises, thought experiments, and discussion topics. Exercises repay repetition; experiments aim to gather evidence, to test or establish proof; topics are places where public debate repeatedly gathers.

Most of your 'missions' will explore specific qualities of videogames as a new entertainment medium alongside broader questions of general human concern. (To be more precise, videogames are not a single physical medium so much as formal structures making varied use of many different media, some dedicated and some multi-purpose.) For much of their short history, videogames have constituted a cultural ghetto in which gamers talk largely amongst themselves using their own jargon. This ghetto still exists to some extent, even though gaming has become more central to popular culture. It's therefore a challenge – some would say an urgent one – for gamers to better understand themselves as part of the historical mainstream of human experience *and* to find how to express this understanding using, so far as possible, non-specialist language that's comprehensible to gamers and non-gamers alike.

Thinking as a discrete activity is particularly associated with Philosophy, probably the oldest of all academic subjects. Yet when considering a young medium like videogames, provocative lines of enquiry arise from many different fields, including Sociology, Psychology, Media and Cultural Studies, as well as History, Film and Literary

Studies. This range reflects much of the emerging syllabus of Game Studies, but in principle *every* discipline can potentially contribute to our understanding of games. Religious Studies, for example, is one of the more recent to recognize that something interesting, from its point of view, is happening in gaming.

Several missions ask you to make a shift in self-awareness by simply noticing what it's like to play a videogame. This might appear slight as a method, but academically has the grand name of phenomenology. It nicely illustrates a basic difference between playing and studying a game: from being fully immersed, you step back somewhat to adopt the position of self-conscious observer.

Even the more armchair-based missions will involve action on your part to bring them alive, since understanding must be embodied as well as intellectual. We learn by doing for ourselves, not just by receiving someone else's knowledge. Reading a recipe is quite different from actually making and tasting the dish described.

Understanding can arrive in a lightning flash or mature over many years. Initiation and rite-of-passage rituals aim to produce dramatic changes in understanding through carefully prepared symbolic acts. Such ceremonies may also serve as formal recognition of a process of change that has been gradually building toward readiness. Some of the missions may function in this way for you.

Finally, several missions ask you to imagine. This is one name for what Rodin's famous sculpture entitled *The Thinker* is doing as he sits frowning, chin on hand. Strictly speaking, to imagine means to form images in your own mind, not just to receive images presented to you. With their digitally-simulated worlds, rendered with ever-greater audiovisual realism, videogames often do much of the imagining for us. In many games we're limited as players to exploring characters, locations, and actions as these have been pre-imagined by the designers. Even the outfits we can choose for our avatar come from a predefined list. Imagination, like invention, is part of creative thinking, reaching into the unknown to bring new shapes and forms into the world. It's therefore important for budding game designers, critics, and educators to activate their own use of this faculty.

Intelligence is a multi-faceted thing, comprising many different mental faculties and subtly adapted to whatever kinds of physical activity a person mostly engages in. Bookish people have a readerly intelligence. They often argue that this is the best and most fundamental kind of all, on the basis that the printed word constitutes the single most efficient means humans have yet discovered of producing and disseminating knowledge. This view is radically challenged by the rise of digital media, especially the Internet and multi-channel broadcasting. Both seem, through the sheer volume of information, viewpoints, and powerful visual images they make available, to produce a more dispersed, less linear, and more visual kind of thinking than books – and a correspondingly different society.

Whether you personally spend more of your time reading books or using social networking software, as a gamer *you become what you do*, in heart and brain, in the same way that a musician, engineer, gardener, athlete, or surgeon does. Thinking is not the goal of their activities, but these activities necessarily shape the way a person doing them thinks. In so far as gaming is one of the main things you do, you cannot help becoming a playthinker. What we don't yet entirely know is, exactly what kind of thinker is that? With the habits it instills, how will gaming enable or constrain your understanding of yourself and the world?

You'll find that the missions follow some basic patterns in their style of presentation but are also quite varied. Sometimes I've identified separate sub-tasks as parts a, b, and c, and these occasionally imply progressive levels of difficulty. The aims of some missions are loosely philosophical (thought experiments and discussion topics) while others have more specific, practical outputs (such as the design-based exercises). The range of missions has been selected in order to provide a spread across the different kinds of activity which I believe would usefully form part of an Introductory Course in Game Studies. This is more or less what you'll get if you read the book from front to back, though you can also choose to focus on those sections that appeal more strongly to your personal interests.

Make some rules

When children make up games, they do little more than invent some rules in response to their current environment. Their ability to do this seems almost inbuilt during a certain phase of their development, starting approximately at the age of five according to child psychologists. After the freeform play of their earlier years, children start to impose arbitrary constraints upon themselves in order to test their intelligence, physical abilities, and social relationships. Us against you, whoever captures most spiders wins. See who can reach the other side of the room first without touching the floor. And if that turns out to be no fun (or you lose) then simply change the rules to create a new game.

What has happened to your childhood creativity? Can you still access it so as to make up a game on the spot?

By definition, a game must have rules. They form a basic contract between all concerned about what is and isn't allowed while playing the game and about how to decide a winner. This is easy to see in sports, board games, card games, and playground games. Soccer's offside rule is notoriously difficult to explain, the box of *Monopoly* contains a printed paper from which players read aloud in moments of dispute, instructions for playing *Top Trumps* fit on to a single card, and around the world groups of schoolchildren negotiate variant rules for playing Tag.

Ask someone to explain the rules of a full-length videogame, however, and they might wonder what you mean.

For example, in the science-fictional, role-playing, third-person shooter game, *Mass Effect* – all those terms required to categorize it tell you this is a genre hybrid, integrating several different types of play – you gradually assemble an élite military squad to defeat an alien superpower. Half of the game's appeal consists in its audiovisual splendor and epic storyline featuring a large cast of characters, exotic locations, and space-operatic themes of humankind's interstellar destiny. From one half hour to the next, gameplay consists of quite different kinds of activity.

In explaining the game, you might therefore highlight key choices, such as whether to make the lead character, Captain Shepard, male or female and an expert with guns or with force fields; some crucial elements of the plot; the morality system whereby you can play either as ethical professional or as corner-cutting rogue; the wheel interface used in combat situations to control your offensive and defensive options; the titular premise of a recently-discovered physical phenomenon, comparable to the force of gravity, which trained specialists can harness in the form of quasi-magical powers... But none of these descriptions feels like 'rules' in the same way as, say, a listing of how each piece is allowed to move in Chess. What each player can do with Shepard and team is much more varied than the repositioning of a knight or queen, and the space of the game's fictional world is larger and more complex than the sixty-four black-and-white squares of the checkerboard.

The fact that players of *Mass Effect* experience the game as a fluid, fictional world, where they can act and achieve goals, testifies to the success of the game's design. It doesn't mean the game's not based on rules, as the definition of a game requires. The fairly detailed manual, though it's not written in the form of a rulebook, effectively is one.

Some of what the player is allowed to do relates to set-dressing rather than functionality. You can give your Captain bleached-blond eyebrows or a bulbous nose, for example, but these changes will affect only your personal attitude towards the character, not how the game behaves or what you must do to complete it. Facial customization is therefore a different kind of rule from, say, the mathematics of how you acquire experience points so as to gain enhanced powers, the prohibitions on walking through walls and off cliffs, and the logic governing dialogue choices, all of which more directly determine what happens in the game.

Everything in the game is programmed, in other words someone had to sit down and write the relevant rules in the form of computer code. Before this stage, however, the design team's first job is to invent a world and interesting things the player can do within it. In practice, their creativity focuses on a few central features that will do the bulk of the work of providing the player with fun. What can the game set the player as challenging tasks capable of being performed over and over in various permutations so it'll feel like there's always something new to do? This is the central question stimulating the game designer's creativity.

Mass Effect offers three main activities (core mechanics): exploration, dialogue, and combat. Each of these takes a distinctive, repetitive form which the player comes to know well. Each has rules that simplify real life and present tasks that are do-able but not too easily or predictably.

A videogame may look and sound beautiful but be let down by its rules. Despite high-resolution graphics and surround sound, players feel they can't do what they'd like, are forced to do what they find boring, or become frustrated by inconsistencies in the game's behavior and logic – whereas videogames may be simple, even crude in appearance and present a very limited range of actions to the player, yet entertain for hours. The highly popular puzzle game series, *Bejewelled*, has become a classic example. You could write its rules on the back of an envelope. Dress up the jewels however you like, the game's success is built on the endless permutations generated according to simple underlying principles so as to exercise and sharpen the player's skills. Similarly Chess, with its apparently simpler rules than *Mass Effect*, nevertheless presents players with greater intellectual challenges through the process known as emergent complexity.

a. Analyze some games and identify their main rules – that is, what they principally allow or forbid the player to do and how they set goals and winning conditions.

So fundamental are rules to any game that this is an alpha-and-omega mission for anyone who wishes to understand videogames better: a key to building expertise based on a lifetime of study, a potential habit of assessment that becomes as second-nature as the restaurant chef's or critic's analysis of flavors and textures in each dish.

How do the game's rules simplify real life so as to produce limited, fun-to-play tasks? What variety of essential and optional actions by players do they enable? What kinds of interaction do they produce between players or between players and the game?

b. Recall your own childhood inventiveness by making up rules for a game based on some everyday activities and objects. Focus on setting one or more aims for the players and limiting how they can go about achieving these. You'll probably find it helpful to think about a genre of game and what kinds of action this usually contains. How do some particular objects behave, what actions can the players perform, what kind of decisions can they make, and what are they disallowed from doing?

Mentally at least, become as carefree, reckless, and imaginative as a child. That chair, turned backwards, is a whinnying horse. Pretend there are no adults around to tell you not to fight, throw food, or jump on the furniture. Without actually playing the game (or only going through some of the motions) begin to test the rules you've invented by envisaging how they might be fun to play. Be prepared to adapt some of the rules to make them interact in more interesting ways.

Then consider how your game might develop as a videogame. How might you visualize the objects and world of the game onscreen using computer graphics? What controls might the player use? And how might the results be more fun than playing using imagination and real-world objects and environments?

Think systematically

Every videogame is a system comprising numerous subsystems, and every part of a videogame is part of at least one of these subsystems.

A system is any set of parts that function together to form a whole. A city's public transport system includes passengers, vehicles, signage, routes, timetables, ticketing, drivers, fuel depots, and so on, all interconnected in a complex organization of which each element has its part to play. The system works provided that each component performs its function in a more-or-less consistent way (or according to the rules, if you like). Along with millions of other commuters, I know only too well what can happen when one part of the transit system fails to perform. A train breaks down, unexpected crowds overwhelm a station, overnight engineering works finish late, drivers are sick, the system struggles and starts to fail.

Systems are all around us, when we look for them. We talk of a weather system, ecosystem, political system, banking system, and educational system, to name just a few.

While each system has its experts, thinking systematically doesn't come naturally. We must step outside our local, individual perspective to understand the bigger picture. We may not like to think we're cogs in a machine or to acknowledge the less pleasant parts of systems from which we benefit – what's required in order to produce a constant stream of cheap consumer goods, say.

Games, computers, and home cinema equipment are sold under the name of systems. They're packages containing parts that we have to unpack and assemble on the living-room floor. In this case the term 'system' has a sophisticated, hi-tech, glamorous air about it – whereas politically 'the system' is often a shorthand term of abuse for oppression of the individual by the State and business corporations.

When we play a videogame, we ourselves become part of a system comprising the game's code (software), the hardware on which the code runs, a power supply, the screen on which we view the game, the input devices we use to control the game, and ourselves as operators. Each of these components is itself a system in various ways: look closer and each is composed of further systems and systems-within-systems. Pursue any one of them and we uncover worlds of wonder and ingenious design.

Consider the game's code. Thousands of hours of skilled human labor have gone into devising the software stored on the game disk. Years of education and work experience went into developing the skills of the various members of the design team. Generations of skilled workers came before them, laying the foundations and passing on knowledge from even earlier generations. To produce those disks required the combined talents of programmers, artists, animators, 3D-modelers, writers, composers, sound engineers, testers, designers, producers, and a host of other specialists. Each worked systematically. All of their work ends up encoded on the disk, packed away into the most compact possible material body of information for convenience of distribution and usage. Not a single person from the development team will be present when you play the game. Everything they've striven for has to work with no further intervention, guaranteed to run. What a feat of design and organization! No wonder glitches and crashes sometimes occur.

When you play a videogame, some of its systems are obvious. For example, the onscreen user interface (HUD, heads-up display) shows information such as health-level, ammunition remaining, and a radar or miniature map. The control system allocates buttons or keys to specific actions in the game. The menu system provides summaries of your assets, missions, discoveries, and so on. Each of these systems has been designed to stay more or less the same throughout the game or to expand to include new content within the initial structure as you progress. In many cases these are what's called extradiegetic systems, in that they don't logically belong within the fictional (diegetic) world of the game.

Other systems are less overt since they do belong within the fictional world. They're integrated smoothly into gameplay so that you don't notice them as separate items. Take the soundtrack, for instance. This is designed to cover every conceivable contingency in the game. Throughout the texture of gameplay there must be information and entertainment for the player's ears, varying moment by moment depending on the circumstances. The development team can't yet produce unique sound effects dynamically on the fly for every individual situation, so these situations must instead be categorized so that a combination of sounds of the appropriate types gets pulled from the disk and played at the right time. Each geographical zone or weather condition has its ambient sounds. Whenever a particular kind of monster approaches, then the sound file for their roar or shriek is played. Whenever your character or vehicle is hit, he, she, or it lets you hear about it in one of several prerecorded ways.

When they're designed well, the systematic behaviors of objects within the game-world are barely noticeable to players who are deeply immersed in the game and familiar with its conventions. You simply know which walls are climbable, which crates can be jumped on top of, what a medical pack looks like, how to aim a grenade, which characters are merely clones, which weapons can or can't penetrate an enemy's shield, and so on.

The *consistency* of any given system is therefore essential both for the designer and for the player. For the designer, having an overall scheme makes the task of producing many component parts manageable. For the player, consistency makes the game learnable and thus a meaningful challenge. If you find, without further explanation, that green bottles, which you've been merrily glugging to regain health, suddenly make you invisible, which is what yellow bottles have previously done, then you're likely to be annoyed with the designers. It's one thing to introduce an element of surprise and confusion by *changing the rules* mid-game, so long as there's a narrative explanation for this and you get the chance to master the new rules. It's another to change the rules with no good reason, apparently through oversight or carelessness.

   a. For any videogame you've played, identify the contributions of any one department within the design team and see how they leave nothing to chance. Every piece should serve a purpose and fit into the whole according to a consistent scheme. The evidence is right there in front of you when you play the game. Pick any element of the game whatsoever. What are the different instances of this element, nearby and throughout the game, that, taken together, form a functioning set, in other words a system? How does this system contribute to making the game as a whole fun to play – or alternatively, if badly designed, to confusing and frustrating the player?

     b. In everyday life you can practice an essential stage in modeling a management simulation by starting to analyze some systems around you – such as the transport system mentioned earlier. Identify the system's functioning parts and the consistent ways in which these behave. How might a player enjoy managing the variables in this system and taking possible corrective actions in case one or more parts begins to fail?

Missions for Thoughtful Gamers

Perform as a human Tic-Tac-Toe machine

This mission presents a rather different kind of activity, designed to give you first-hand understanding of computation.

What you'll need
10 sheets of card
1 marker pen
2 sticks for pointing
2 people to play a game on you

Preparation
1. Take a sheet of card and with the marker pen write out the following message: 'Welcome to the human Tic-Tac-Toe machine. Click anywhere to begin.' On the reverse, write the number 1.
2. Take a second card and draw out the usual three-by-three grid of squares. Number this card 2. Make two more copies of this card so the players can replay the game (best of three).
3. On another card write: 'Player A moves.' Mark this number 3.
4. On another: 'Player B moves.' Mark this number 4.
5. On another: 'Player A wins, congratulations! Player B loses, too bad! Play again? Y / N'. Mark this number 5.
6. On another: 'Player B wins, congratulations! Player A loses, too bad! Play again? Y / N'. Mark this number 6.
7. On another: 'It's a draw! Play again? Y / N'. Mark this number 7.
8. On another: 'Goodbye.' Mark this number 8.
9. Take one of the sticks and mark the end so that you can distinguish one stick from the other. Decide which stick you'll treat as Player A and which as Player B.
10. Read the following rules, which you'll operate during the game.

11. Arrange the room as follows. Find somewhere to present the sheets of card and for you to sit or stand with your back turned to the players. You'll communicate with them by presenting or marking the relevant cards. They'll communicate with you by pointing with their sticks. You'll need to see which stick is pointing and where. Place the sticks ready for the players to use.

Rules
1. Present the card numbered 1. When either player 'clicks' the card with their stick, remove card 1.
2. Present a blank card 2.
3. Present card 3 alongside card 2.
4. If player B clicks, ignore this.
5. Note where player A clicks.
    a. If player A clicks on a square that's already filled, or outside the grid, ignore this.
    b. If player A clicks on a blank square, with your marker pen enter an X in the relevant square on card 2.
6. Check to see if there are three Xs in a row.
    a. If there are, remove cards 2 and 3, display card 5, then go to step 10.
    b. If there aren't, replace card 3 with card 4.
7. If player A clicks, ignore this.
8. Note where player B clicks.
    a. If player B clicks on a square that's already filled, or outside the grid, ignore this.
    b. If player B clicks on a blank square, mark an O in the relevant square on card 2.
9. Check to see if there are three Os in a row.
    a. If there are, remove cards 2 and 3, display card 6, then go to step 10.
    b. If there aren't, check to see if this is the last possible move (the grid is full).
        i. If it isn't, replace card 4 with card 3, then go to step 4.
        ii. If it is, replace card 4 with card 7, then go to step 10.

Missions for Thoughtful Gamers

10. Note where either player clicks.
    a. If either player clicks on Y, go to step 2.
    b. If either player clicks on N, replace card 5/6 with card 8.

<u>Play</u>

Invite the players to approach the game. Direct them to the sticks and then adopt your chosen position for operating the game. Answer any initial questions the players may have, then follow the Rules given above. Operate in silence or devise a system of beeps to emit for each type of move by the players.

Assuming you know this game well, from childhood, you should have little difficulty in acting as the players' glorified pen. And once you're familiar with the various cards and the general procedure, you should perform smoothly at displaying or removing the appropriate card.

Imagine, though, that you had *no prior knowledge of the game*. You must then operate the rules mechanically with no other understanding of what they mean. That's exactly how a computer or game console works, by blindly (and very quickly) following carefully-crafted instructions. You've performed as a human computer by following a logical procedure of steps designed to anticipate all possible moves, contingencies, and outcomes.

In outline, what's given above are the bare bones of a videogame program (not an especially elegant one, I daresay). Tic-Tac-Toe was turned into arguably the first videogame, back in the 1950s on a primitive early computer, and it's still used as a first exercise for game programmers precisely because of its simplicity. Merely figure out how to reproduce the above procedure electronically, together with an extended program enabling a single player to play against the computer (you) instead of another human, and hey presto! you've a videogame.

For a further challenge, start to work out how you might perform as a human Reversi (Othello) machine.

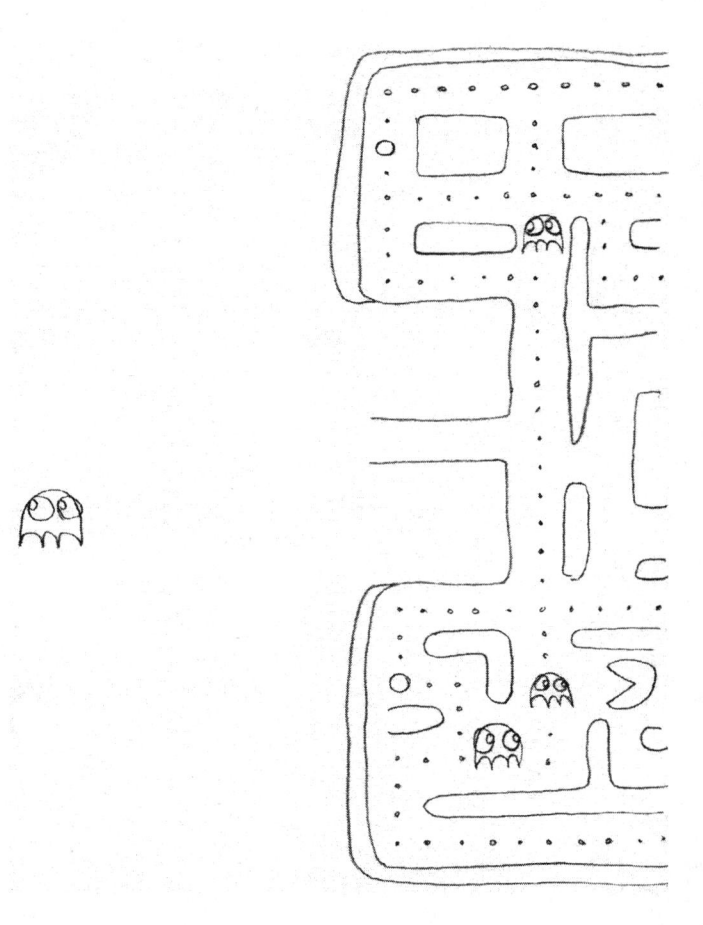

EPISODE 1:
HIDDEN LANDS

Episode 1: Hidden Lands

Videogames as enquiry

You ain't seen nothing yet. Or at least we can reasonably expect videogames in the future to do many things they've not yet done. In the early twenty-first century they're a young cultural form (despite humankind's millennia of play) in the same way that cinema was in the early twentieth and the novel in the late eighteenth. At this point in their growth and evolution, we're still finding out what videogames can do.

Our interest is as much in their technology and formal properties as in their content. As Marshall McLuhan observed regarding television in the 1960s, conservatives tend to worry about the content of a new medium – how it represents sex and violence, say, which have lost their shock-value in older media. They fail to see that the greater impact consists in the mere fact of the medium's presence within the cultural and sensory field. Everything else must move over and adjust to the new personality in the room.

Content is nevertheless important. Every creative medium finds its own way of exploring and responding to the phenomenal richness of reality. For commercial reasons, mainstream games tend to make the most of certain conventionalized fantasies, identifiable more or less by genre: stealth shooter, sport simulation, real-time military strategy, and so on. But innovation in the game industry, at its best, is also fuelled among other things by a spirit of enquiry into the sheer variety of human experience. Within the foreseeable future we might hope videogames will shed their image of intellectual thinness and become more thoroughly engaged with thinking, in their own way, about the 'real world' in all its material, social, and philosophical variety.

Currently, mainstream commercial games catering for mass markets must deliver pleasures mostly of relatively familiar and instant kinds. A majority focus on scenarios of combat and conquest in one form or another – whether it's a cartoonish children's game or a gory mature (18) certificate shooter. The narrowness of videogames' themes, characters, and ambitions is a familiar complaint, often made as part of a larger attack on an allegedly juvenile, irresponsible, escapist, and even dangerous medium. Sometimes it appears that 'progress' in videogames means little more than improved graphics, celebrated in marketing hype for the latest installment of an already-successful franchise.

Game production and publishing have nevertheless for many years been a professional industry operating in competitive international entertainment markets. Standards of production, creativity, and technological development are now generally very high across the sector. Among gamers, theoretical and critical discussions have advanced considerably over the last ten years, leaving many non-gamers behind, ill-informed. Independent and avant-garde game scenes have emerged, though not yet so substantial or well-organized as world and art-house cinema, say. The serious and educational games movements have made some progress in promoting the development of videogames that function as agents of social and political change rather than purely for entertainment or profit. Within the last few years, casual and downloadable games for new platforms such as smart telephones have begun to enable a wider range of people to become involved in development. With their small budgets, these games also allow for forms of creative experimentation that are often stifled by corporate caution over the large-scale investment required for full-length games.

Many real-world and historical subjects do appear to remain off-limits for today's major game studios. Should a mainstream developer want to set a full-length videogame in an intensive-care ward, ballet school, abattoir, Native American reservation, Norwegian whaling village, eighteenth-century slave-trading ship, or World-War-One trench, say, either the publishers will query its commercial viability or moral conservatives will cry outrage. Some such settings might feature briefly in games, but not, I think, with any depth of realism or historical detail. (Partly this reflects the current dominance of American developers and markets, who are more interested, for example, in the American Civil War than the French Revolution.)

By contrast, every subject under the sun is now fair game for novelists, including most controversially true crime and traumatic public events such as natural disasters and terrorist attacks. Game developers will one day enjoy the same freedom of subject matter, we might reasonably assume.

Not all videogames have a 'subject,' however. What makes puzzle games enjoyable are their underlying algorithms – the rules and formulae which determine each player's success and failure from moment to moment and over the course of the game. The pieces of the puzzle may remain highly abstract, yet working out how to move them is intensely fun. Likewise a platforming game might nominally be set in a conventional gothic mansion, but primarily be pleasurable for some particularly well-designed running and jumping tasks. The setting could then be altered (modded) and little would be lost.

Still, we can legitimately wonder how game developers might be inspired to generate new algorithms and new core mechanics through researching real-world settings. The grand historical projects of the sciences, which aim to discover the laws of nature, in principle encompass *all* phenomena. Their curiosity is systematic. These projects provide the knowledge base for many videogame algorithms, whether it's the economic model underpinning *SimCity*'s urban-planning simulator, the physics engine determining the semi-realistic behavior of a skidding car in a *Formula 1* racing game, or the artificial intelligence governing the tactics of alien soldiers in the bestselling shooter series, *Halo*.

Over the centuries many artists, too, have displayed an ambitious appetite of enquiry. This has resulted in new ways to perceive the world and our subjective experience of it. Thus videogames have recapitulated a centuries-long history of experimentation in visual representation, most obviously in the use of axonometric projection, perspective, and cinematic photorealism.

We should expect videogames to play a role in continuing to evolve our ways of perceiving and understanding our place in the world. Game developers and industry pundits are constantly looking for the Next Big Thing. Often this is envisaged in primarily technological terms, such as the production of enhanced graphical capabilities and more responsive motion controllers. But an equally potent basis for change lies in the ambition of players and developers to better understand themselves and the wide, wide world. The following missions sample some ways you might do this so as to explore possible new sources of design concepts.

Turn your life-story into an autobiogame

It's a familiar fantasy question: who would star in the Hollywood movie of your life? Choose any leading lady or man you like – money is no object – to play you. Only this time it will be a videogame, not a film.

Potentially there can be as many autobiogames as there are individuals in the world. We know that, in practice, only a few lives are selected for public celebration, but just for now let's imagine that one of them is yours.

To start with something seemingly mundane, consider what mini-games you might base on your hobbies and interests, everyday pleasures and annoyances. Which aspects of your daily existence could be fun to play? Look at what you did this morning, yesterday, or last weekend. If you were a Sim, from the famous Maxis game, what were the activities the player instructed your character to do today around the home, in the street, at work, and at play?

Check in with this exercise when you wake up, on your way out in the morning, at lunchtime, on your way home, right up until the moment you go to bed. Allow your perception of the day's routine and events to become filtered by this fantasy. Monitor how your day, as you actually live it, feels game-like. If you're a frequent gamer, then games are inside your body and mind, so how do they wait to come out while you're fixing breakfast, making a 'phone call, or walking the dog?

There's a larger point, however. Biopics and biographies always dramatize the storyline of their individual subject's life. What have been peak moments or rites of passage when life presented you with particularly enjoyable or challenging experiences? What have been some highs and lows of the personal emotional rollercoaster you've been riding? What kind of hero will your preferred actor play you as being? In what pose will he or she appear in the game's marketing poster? How will the player progress through the game, and towards what goals? Who in your life has taken the role of opponent, and what will the player of the game-of-your-life achieve by overcoming all obstacles? I hope no-one has actually been as big a villain towards you as you might exaggerate them to be in the game.

Focus on a significant period in your past, aspects of your present-day life and how you hope it'll turn out, or imagine a point some time in your future. Maybe experiment with an alternative version of your life's story, one which took a different turn as a result of a key decision or stroke of chance. How will your story end – in the game, that is? The game might be lighthearted and uplifting or dark and serious. Be true to reality or use poetic license as you see fit.

There's not yet an equivalent videogame genre to biopics and biographies, where you get to play a famous historical person's life, though such figures do of course feature in games. You'll still have plenty of models of what a life-story should be. Celebrity culture and religion, for example, propose very different visions of how to 'win' at life, based on achieving fame and material wealth or living righteously and with faith.

Some have wondered whether our lives actually *are* being played, right this minute, by someone else: a god, a government agent, or an extraterrestrial being. Especially cruel accidents and twists of fate make you wonder whether the person upstairs actually enjoys seeing you suffer, is bored, or just a rubbish player. Philosophically there's an old idea here. 'As flies to wanton boys are we to the gods; They kill us for their sport,' complains one of the characters in Shakespeare's *King Lear*. His personal suffering makes him pessimistic about humans' ability to control their own future (free will) and skeptical about divine love and justice. Having created the universe, the supreme being treats it as his toy. Greek mythology, too, suggests the gods enjoy playing with mortals. In the 1981 film *Clash of the Titans* the Olympians of ancient Greece are shown using miniature humans as pieces in a game of Chess.

Existentialist philosophy, by contrast, urges us to reject the idea that any external agent judges or defines the meanings of our lives. What matters is that each individual takes responsibility for how he or she chooses to live. We're free to create our own rules and winning conditions. This doesn't mean we can simply go around being nasty to people. Rather, we should make important life-choices more consciously as morally free agents, not as victims or dependents of our parents, marketing campaigns, the government, or a church.

If your autobiogame is not to be a clone of numerous others, then you must discover how your life can be authentically yours. Return to the knowledge that it's yours still to live. As a person learns from writing their autobiography, how might imagining your autobiogame enable you to understand – and therefore live – your life differently?

Missions for Thoughtful Gamers

Engame the gamer

Films about film directors, novels about novelists, stage plays about actors, songs about singers, television dramas about television executives... So why not also videogames about game developers and gamers?

We enjoy seeing what goes on behind the scenes of any creative industry, not only through fly-on-the-wall documentaries but also in fictionalized accounts which show people as heroes and villains. We want to know the intrigues, romances, scandals, disasters, battles, triumphs, daily trials, sorrows, and joys of life in the art and entertainment business. But there's an additional curiosity when the commentary occurs within the medium that's at stake. When an art-form turns its gaze upon itself, a kind of giddy confusion occurs, like the effect of receding reflections in opposed mirrors or Escher's black-and-white drawing of two hands drawing each other. (With a stricter application, this is called *mise-en-abyme*.)

The self-portrait is perhaps the oldest example. The painter scrutinizes himself, warts and all, or attempts to define his iconic public image. In modern terminology, reflexivity – looking back at yourself – has become a central principle in many fields. How can you teach, nurse, or criticize without a degree of self-awareness about the principles you're applying? Physician, heal thyself.

Self-reference is also a distinguishing feature of so-called postmodern popular culture and arts. It's often humorous and sometimes thought-provoking. The heroine of a television sitcom looks out of the screen directly at the viewer and jokes how the plot's mistreating her (breaking the so-called fourth wall). Or a celebrity makes a cameo appearance in a soap opera only for the cast to slyly tease about a recent real-life scandal. A music video by an international pop star with a long career ironically 'quotes' an image famous from one of her earliest music videos. All these devices require that we are knowing audiences, thoroughly familiar with the conventions of the particular form and able to spot references to other popular texts or to the prior history of a show or star.

As in the worst examples of obscure academic writing, self-referentiality in postmodern popular culture and arts can become stale and tedious, a self-indulgent conversation with itself, empty of any substantial content and often given the bad name of navel-gazing.

As with movies about producers, directors, actors, and all the rest of the many people who contribute to making a film, so a videogame about itself could feature as heroes, allies, and villains all those who work in a game development studio or publishing house. You play a programmer, 3D-modeler, lead designer, producer, sound engineer, tester, or someone in the personnel or accounts department. What's your mission, and what kinds of thing will the player do as you?

For now, I suggest, many of us have little idea, in so far as the insides of the game industry are relatively unknown to gamers and even more so to non-gamers. Hence Kairosoft's casual game, *Game Dev Story*, is a management simulation, unable to show us any inner lives of the development team. As yet, we have almost no public mythology for this world in the way we do for, say, the worlds of rock music and sport. Imagining a videogame about the game industry, we have few legends or famous personalities from which to begin.

How might you as a gamer also feature as the hero in a game about videogames? Unlike movies, where the viewer can do nothing to affect the outcome of what happens on screen, players are actively involved throughout a game in making things happen (even if this is somewhat an illusion). This experience of playing could itself become the subject of a game.

Towards the end of the stealth shooter *Metal Gear Solid 2: Guns of the Patriots*, an onscreen interface that the player has been using throughout the game unexpectedly jams. A message appears saying that the game has crashed. This isn't true. The crash is a simulation. The effect is disorienting because the game suddenly addresses the player as if from outside its fictional world. We might say it induces a momentary paranoia, as the world that's previously been kept safely inside the game threatens to break into the room where you sit with controller in hand before the screen. In such a moment, one might imagine fictional characters within the game knocking at your door and hurrying you onto the streets outside your window to help complete for real the mission you were a moment ago playing onscreen.

This kind of imaginative leap, ridiculous when viewed rationally, is a well-known effect aimed at in horror genres. It's sometimes called the uncanny. There are also many comparable examples of comic effect, since disorientation can make us laugh as well as shrink in fear.

When gamers do feature as major characters in fiction and films, they're typically science-fictional heroes uniquely able to move between the real and virtual or in-game worlds. This character type, appearing most recently in the film *Gamer*, derives from the computer hackers of *Tron* and *The Matrix*, only now the hero must be a master of 3D gaming instead of programming. Curiously, perhaps, this figure has yet to appear with any frequency in videogames themselves. And surely it's not the only figure we can imagine?

Everyday gamers in their everyday lives make relatively few appearances as major characters in films, television dramas, or documentaries. This leaves the field open for videogames not just to tell gamers' stories but also (dizzying prospect) to allow us to *play* gamers' adventures, comprising events occurring half in the real world and half in the virtual.

Re-center a game's cultural perspective

Many countries have a national literature, cinema, music, cuisine, dress, and other art-forms. These are based, among other things, on the country's history and landscape, its ethnic and religious composition, its intellectual and folk traditions. Out from these roots, why shouldn't more countries also grow a national videogaming style and content to set alongside those of America and Japan? What might the equivalent of Bollywood videogames be like, for example?

Currently videogames form part of America's empire as the world's only cultural, economic, military, and political superpower. As its movies dominate English-speaking film production, and its television is sold to channels worldwide, so its videogames flood the shelves of game shops in many countries. In gaming, Japan is its only major rival. Compared to these two giants, no other country has a national game industry of global significance. Geographically game production is spread across many countries, including the United Kingdom, Canada, France, and Korea, but none of these has successfully exported a powerful gaming brand expressive of their national culture. Ask a gamer in Sydney or Hamburg, for example, to name a distinctively British videogame. For that matter, conduct a straw poll of gamers in London and see how many they can name.

This is important in so far as entertainment produced for mass consumption, even apparently innocuous forms such as pop music and lifestyle magazines, adds up to a pervasive, subtle influence on people's values, attitudes, and behavior (in other words, a vehicle of ideology).

Globalization is a two-edged sword. On the one side, everywhere is becoming increasingly the same – some would say, Americanized. International corporations and financial organizations seem to have more power than national governments; you can walk into the same big-brand stores in towns and cities around the world to buy the same pair of jeans or order an identically-tasting burger; the same blockbuster movies fill cinemas in Helsinki, Cape Town, and Buenos Aires; and billions speak some version of English. Yet on the other side, mass media allow us to experience as never before the vast diversity of cultures around the world. More than in any previous century, we have opportunities to appreciate the sheer variety of human life as well as to recognize the extent of our shared, common humanity. Albeit in a packaged form, you or I can sample food, music, dance, dress, language, customs, art, architecture, natural wonders, and more, from almost any region on Earth, from Mexico to Tibet, from Syria to Iceland.

Much of this sampling is secondhand, shallowly touristic, and potentially exploitative. Indigenous peoples have therefore wised up to the importance of asserting ownership over their cultural property and of using cultural exchange for educational and political purposes. In Australia, cooperatives of Aboriginal artists create community income through sales of 'dot paintings.' Native American beadwork products are often sold with accompanying information about tribal history.

At a local level, many if not most people have a stake in some battle or other that has to be fought against the powerful forces that govern our world. Wherever there's conflict, injustice, oppression, prejudice, disadvantage, exclusion, misrepresentation, or misunderstanding, videogames are a potential vehicle through which to campaign or simply express a point of view that's otherwise unrecognized. The serious games movement already tackles a variety of social and political issues, including environmental damage and the effects of war. But judging from the history of other media, such as television drama, we might expect videogames, especially as their creation becomes open to a wider range of makers, to increasingly explore diversity of opinion and cultural perspective, not just as worthy academic projects, but as provocative entertainment. (We should expect this to include expression of views we may personally disagree with or even find offensive.)

a. Identify any stereotyped character in an existing videogame and explore what the game might look like when viewed from his or her perspective, brought into central position. This requires you to understand, or at least imagine, this character's experience as being as valid as the usual hero's. What are the character's history, origins, motivations, conflicts, hopes, and aims? What's it like to be this person? In most cases the existing game will provide only limited information on these points, so you'll need to research and invent.

b. What opportunities are there in some particular videogames to play consciously *as* a person with a specific cultural identity? Even when a game allows you to customize your character's physical appearance and other features, this is usually only skin-deep. You can play as a dark-skinned female, but not as a Black woman aware of what her race and gender mean in her society – nor as a person with a particular religious faith, ethnicity, sexual orientation, or disability. How might such an option be designed into the game, and what would need to change for this to occur? Rather than assuming the result must be commercially unviable, how might it produce new kinds of enjoyable and satisfying experience for players?

c. Which elements of your own cultural identity might find expression in a videogame? How could your sense of, say, regional identity (that part of your country from which you or your ancestors originate or to which you now belong) act as source for a game's stories, characters, myths, settings, visual or musical influences? Which key images might you select to showcase as representing an identity you share with many others, and how might these lead players towards a deeper understanding and respect?

Missions for Thoughtful Gamers

Try Surrealism

Here's a simple way to start. When the French Surrealists invented the procedure at the start of the twentieth century, they called it Exquisite Corpse. You may have played a version of it as a child.

Each player takes a sheet of paper and at the top of the page draws a head with two stalks to show where the neck ends. Each player folds the paper so the head is turned over and can't be seen, then passes the paper to the player on their left. Players now draw the shoulders, arms, and torso, fold the paper again so these can't be seen, and pass it on. Continue with this process down to the legs and finally the feet. At the end of the process, reveal the composite characters.

Your objective here is to produce new videogame characters. If you're good at drawing you could follow the process above. Alternatively, you could find images of characters online; print them out, ideally at approximately the same scale; cut each into four sections (head, torso, legs, feet); place these component parts into piles; randomly pick one piece from each pile in turn and use these to assemble the character. Or just write down relevant names on pieces of paper, slot these at random into the four body positions, and use your imagination to visualize the result.

If this is too complicated, a simplified version consists in head-swapping. The potency of this procedure is proven by the animal-headed (theriomorphic) deities of Hinduism and ancient Egypt.

There's no reason why you should restrict yourself entirely to videogame characters. As well as animals, you could include celebrities, household objects, and frankly anything else that comes to mind. So be it if the character turns out as a nonsensical mixture of human, animal, and machine. That's cyborgs for you.

When you look at the results and start to select those which are more successful than others, your guides should be humor, artistic intuition, and the logic of dreams. You might as well be looking at the work of someone intoxicated or insane. Any combination that whispers from your unconscious is worth pursuing. You could edit the results so they make more sense – taming them, so to speak – or in true Surrealist spirit value the very weirdness of whatever has been produced by the randomizing process. Positively prefer what's most disturbing, bizarre, and absurd. Actively seek it out. Your aim is to break free from the confines that rationality places upon the imagination and to bypass convention. Creativity here arises not from careful planning and skilful execution but from flashes of insight – furtive joy – as you survey the jumble of images.

What is the composite character's name? Perhaps combine selected syllables from the original characters' names to form a new one. What are the character's personality traits and special abilities, likes and dislikes? How will he, she, or it move and fight? Use your imagination and your knowledge of games to develop ideas from the initial starting point: bring the exquisite corpse, the Frankenstein monster, more fully to life. Also consider some of the resulting composite characters side-by-side to discover which might become either teammates or enemies.

Try a similar randomized sampling process with other elements, such as game environments, mechanics, and storylines. For example, intercut the settings of different kinds of game – battlefield, spaceship, racetrack, jungle, motel, and so on – to create new composite spaces. Which kinds of game might happen inside the resulting locations? How would your composite characters interact with these environments, and what missions would they pursue there?

At first, the Surrealist approach will seem not much more than its popular image, namely a parlor game capable of producing little of real value. You may be reminded of the many ways such methods have already been assimilated into contemporary (postmodern) culture. Sampling and zaniness are no longer radical. Aren't we just talking *Super Smash Bros. Brawl* and *WarioWare*, for example?

As a game designer, artist, critic, or educator, you will not allow these first impressions to deter you. If the above methods once succeed in sparking your imagination they'll have proved their worth. Original creative power is true gold-dust, stranger, rarer, and more dangerous than 'how to' books on creativity and game design might have you believe.

> In the guise of civilization, under the pretext of progress, we have succeeded in dismissing from our minds anything that, rightly or wrongly, could be regarded as superstition or myth; and we have proscribed every way of seeking the truth which does not conform to convention.
> – André Breton, 'The Manifesto of Surrealism' (1924)

Episode 1: Hidden Lands

Auralize an audiogame

It was a bright weekday morning. London's river Thames flowed past, busy with tourist boats, to the dull hum of road traffic crossing Waterloo Bridge. I turned and entered a doorway that I'd never noticed before, beneath one of the concrete walkways. After paying for my ticket I joined a huddle of intrepid visitors. Moments later and we were edging cautiously into pitch-black darkness. I held the hand of the stranger in front, and someone else held on behind me. Up ahead the voice of our blind guide waited to help us cross a busy road, and later we made our way into a pub – an aural-tactile simulation of one, that is.

For me this was a fascinating experience. As you'd expect, my senses of sound and touch heightened. I found myself imagining the space around me using aural and tactile cues in place of the usual visual ones. Rather than mentally visualizing the space, in the short visit (even my sense of time began to change, as I recall) I developed a mental map of the unseen street that was based on my memories of sound and touch. I auralized and tactilized it, so to speak.

The 'video' in videogames means 'I see,' from the Latin verb *videre*. What of our other senses? Could they become the center of gameplay?

Probably there's a limit to what we'll ever be able to do in designing gustogames and olfaceogames (*gustare*, to taste; *olfacere*, to smell). Our most primitive senses are powerful but normally capable of articulation only through specialist training, such as received by the professional wine taster and perfumer. We cannot play detective smelling games as police sniffer dogs might do. In his adventure at Arkham Asylum, Batman follows various scent-trails, but these must be visualized for the player. Though laboratory chemists can reproduce specific aromas synthetically, these can't be delivered in a nimble sequence of sensations in the manner of a musical tune or pattern of colored lights. Cinema's experiment with releasing scents into the auditorium to accompany particular scenes was notoriously short-lived.

Tangeogames (*tangere*, to touch) are more feasible. Human cultures have devised many systems for training and applying the sense of touch. Skilled musicians can play with eyes closed. Braille offers a complete system for reading by touch. Combined with sight, touch and movement are essential to using the vast majority of everyday devices, including videogame controllers. The latter have long been a focus of research and development, most recently in terms of motion-sensitive controllers, such as the Wii remote, Xbox Kinect, and tilt-games on mobile-phone touch-screens, which have opened up various kinds of movement as a major extension of visual play. Ideally game controllers produce the illusion that you're directly manipulating objects within the game. Often this aims to feel fluid and easy, like the nonchalant movements of experts. On other occasions you must take more care, like a scientist using precise robotic arms to manipulate sensitive items inside a glass case.

Videogames already simulate a fair range of tactile actions in the real world. These tend to focus on popular genres of gameplay and readily simplifiable actions, such as steering a car and pointing a gun, which emphasize deft use of devices via controls. How might a game also simulate actions where the hands themselves are the implements and present these actions as simplified challenges of progressive difficulty: kneading bread, sculpting clay, giving someone a shoulder massage, weeding by hand, folding laundry… or are such manual actions beneath all interest?

Tangeogames would emphasize touching over looking as the main thing the player must learn to do. They might include graphics and be a multisensory feast, as many videogames are, or offer more austere monosensory pleasure. Some videogame controllers use vibration to provide directly tactile cues to the player. These are crude, though, compared to the number and sophistication of visual and aural cues coming from the screen and speakers. Imagine instead a more protean (shape-changing) device, functioning in place of the screen as the main focus of attention and capable of simulating rough and smooth, hot and cold, wet and dry, as well as motion. Closing her eyes, the player enters a world of touch where the most interesting tasks are tactile.

Episode 1: Hidden Lands

If tangeogames are difficult to imagine (tactilise as a sequence of touch-images), audiogames are somewhat easier. Indeed they already comprise an existing genre, many examples of which are available online. Games centered on sound are not just for blind gamers. Sound gives us many pleasures as well as practical ability to function in the world. Along with sight, hearing is one of our most physiologically developed senses, providing a large share of our information about the world. Human civilization would be impossible without speech and the written language derived from it. Conversation, oratory, drama, and music are among our chief arts. Many people fear the prospect of growing deaf.

Sound attracts research and development attention from the industry and academics, but still trails behind graphics. Rather than dismissing audiogames as a minor niche market, we could explore sound further as potentially fertile territory for mainstream gaming.

With singing and rhythm games it might seem that we already have sound-centered games. This is only partly true. Observing a group playing *Guitar Hero*, I asked them to try a song with the sound turned off. Bemused, they succeeded but declared it to be less fun – though they laughed more than when the sound was turned up, presumably because they were thrown back to being clumsy beginners again. On their own the sound cues don't give the player sufficient information to complete a song, so that to do so with sound up but blindfolded a player would need to memorize it first via visually-aided play-throughs.

Imagine a development studio where teams of composers, linguists, sound engineers, voice actors, and ex-radio dramatists outnumber or displace altogether the teams of artists, 3D-modelers, animators, and motion-capture specialists. The physics team will spend their time modeling the behavior of sound in the real world, how it bounces, diffuses, and distorts. The game's hero might be a blind or partially-sighted character who uses an acute sense of hearing, musical and linguistic knowledge to navigate the world and complete missions. Perhaps the player will train to become like the ninja who's deadly even when blindfolded and stuns with a high-pitched shriek, or the hunter who hears a deer's tread from across the valley and imitates the calls of different birds.

 a. Regularly sit still, close your eyes, and focus on listening to your environment. Practice identifying the key features that define it as a distinctive sound space. Develop your sense of hearing so that it becomes more acute – imagine you're a bat or other sharp-eared animal. Think about what you hear as if you're a detective. Allow yourself to respond emotionally to what you hear. Store to memory a mental soundtrack of the place comprising all of the above.

 b. Listen to someone playing a videogame. Without seeing what's happening onscreen, imagine as best you can the environment and action. Take a favorite game you know intimately and try to play some of it with your eyes closed or back turned, based on your memories and the sound cues.

 c. Consider in turn some typical core game mechanics from different genres, such as targeting, steering, jumping, choosing dialogue options, spell-casting, combining combat movements, directing items upon a terrain, and so on. How could each of these be presented as a challenge requiring the player to listen instead of look, to make a noise instead of move controls? What might be the fun in this?

Spot stories that want to be games

It's now commonplace for action-adventure movies to prepare the ground for a tie-in videogame. Sometimes you wonder whether the film is just a glorified game-trailer, so strongly do whole scenes, one after the other, anticipate videogame levels. Thus James Bond completes a series of small-scale and spectacular action sequences – infiltrating a foreign embassy, escaping from a car chase, fighting off and eventually killing his would-be assassin, disarming a ticking bomb with seconds to spare – punctuated by calmer moments of dialogue, tourism, and seduction.

Bond movies were ever thus. What's happened is that videogames now seem to define the pattern that 007's adventures must live up to.

Not just Bond, any action hero or heroine: Indiana Jones, Charlie's Angels, Jason Bourne…

Not just action heroes and heroines, either. The influence of videogames' level- and mission-based structure reaches into crime, police procedurals, and forensic investigations whether these occur on the page, on the stage, or on the screen. Solving the mystery, bringing felons to justice, and keeping the streets clean each breaks down into sub-tasks, such as interviewing witnesses and informants, examining the murder-scene for evidence, and raiding a hideout. In turn each of these is potentially a playable level or part of one. Complete the sequence of missions and our sleuths are led to the climactic showdown and revelation: I might be describing a videogame, a detective novel, or a murder-mystery weekend, despite the substantial differences between these.

Much the same could be said of Tolkeinesque sword 'n' sorcery, caped-crusading superheroes' battles against evil masterminds, demon-slaying, or science fiction horror. Each of these genres functions across multiple entertainment media, and videogames provide a powerful master-model for their structure.

Even when there's no likelihood of a videogame tie-in, we might expect the level- and mission-based structure increasingly to function across the board as an implicit, popular understanding of how a well-told story or well-constructed drama is organized. So-called chick-lit, for example, which typically follows the careers and love-lives of girls-about-town, belongs in the genre of women's romantic fiction, which is ostensibly far removed from videogames. Yet its characters and readers may well include gamers (casual or not-so casual), and how else are their fictional and real-life adventures to be structured if not into levels and missions? Aren't career progression and love both games, after all – of winners and losers, where all's fair as it is in war? In Japan, the dating sim is an established genre.

In order to win her man, romantic-comedy heroine Bridget Jones must complete a series of principally dialogue-based flirtation and courtship missions. Most of these consist in comically embarrassing failure, as do her attempts to resist fattening foods, alcohol, and cigarettes. In the original newspaper serialization and novelization, daily diary entries structure the story. In the subsequent film adaptations, the diary form, which belongs on the printed page, gives way to a dramatic structure comprising scenes and linking sequences, two-handed dialogues, and multi-character set-pieces. By migrating from page to screen, Bridget's story moves towards videogames' sphere of influence. You've read her diary, watched her adventures onscreen, now play as Jones!

According to one myth of videogames, this most modern of entertainment media shows us the *future of interactive narrative and drama*, towards which all previous forms of storytelling have been aspiring. Whatever their current limitations, videogames establish a widespread populist desire to *play* characters and roles more directly than readers and audiences have been able to do in the past. It follows that every hit title in all the older media must want in principle to become a videogame, to inspire a breakthrough in this form or fail in the attempt.

As I said, this is the logic of a myth – though it's possible the myth might one day be at least partly fulfilled. For the moment there are clear limits to videogames' actual influence on perceptions of narrative pattern and dramatic structure. Novelists, scriptwriters, and playwrights each work first and foremost with the proven techniques specific to their medium. Keen theater-goers and comic-book fans may have little sense of videogame structure, or indeed none whatsoever. On the other hand, the direction of change in popular culture is currently towards greater influence for videogames, as gamers become more numerous across multiple generations and as games themselves advance in their technology and design.

This influence is not limited to fictional narratives. Televised sports events are now shadowed by their simulations in videogames. NATO's smart-guided missiles and remotely-controlled drones, as seen in television news stories, can give the impression of turning war into a videogame.

As you keep watch for stories-that-want-to-be-games, begin to consider some of the practical questions concerning the hypothetical task of adaptation from one medium to another. Which parts of the story might be fun to play? How could a mission- and level-structure apply? Which genre of game would the adaptation be? Which parts of the original could stay more or less as they are and which would need to be radically changed?

You might also consider some wider implications. What does the gamelike quality of a particular story reveal about the shifting power-relations between videogames and more established, culturally high-status media? What might be the ethical consequences of treating a non-fictional story as a form of entertainment?

Conceive a Holocaust, civilian, or pacifist war game

Auschwitz or Hiroshima, Nazi death-camp or A-bomb inferno, the extremes of human brutality and destructive power are alike off-limits for commercial videogames. Here lies true horror, no grounds for 'fun.' The only ethical artistic response to such monstrous realities is to present them with searing honesty or devastating satire in the hope of preventing them from ever happening again. *Sophie's Choice* and *Dr Strangelove* show how cinema has risen to this challenge. The graphic novels *Maus* and *Barefoot Gen* are equally powerful and belie critics who dismiss comics as a juvenile form. Can videogames do something similar?

Here's one argument why videogames, at least as they're currently designed, might be incapable *in principle* of addressing the European Holocaust. (It's made by Gonzalo Frasca in his essay 'Ephemeral Games: Is it Barbaric to Design Video Games after Auschwitz?' which is available online.) Imagine a game in which the player takes the part of a prisoner in a concentration camp. The game's designers intend this fictional experience to be morally educative. Through the scenes they witness and the revealed consequences of their actions, players will be caused to think about what it means to survive such an environment, about ethical choice, and about core human values. However, the designers must then make it possible for players to perform morally bad actions, such as betraying fellow prisoners. Even if the game shows this to be a losing strategy, some players will choose to perform such actions anyway – for the fun of it. In other words the videogame will become a 'simulator for sadists.' The dominant convention whereby a player can easily restart a section of the game, for example by loading from a Save point, will enable players to experiment with atrocious behavior. The death of a fellow prisoner will mean nothing if it can be undone by simply reloading the game.

More straightforwardly, we can say that the simplistic concept of winning and losing, which structures many commercial videogames, is morally abhorrent when applied to the appalling experience of imprisonment in a concentration camp. As Primo Levi and other Holocaust survivors have testified, those who lived to escape the camps were not 'winners.'

The glut of World War II shooters and combat simulators, either blithely unrealistic or pretending to historical accuracy, allows players to act out conventional scenarios of military heroism over and over. These games are always morally simplistic to a greater or lesser degree: win the shootout, out-maneuver and annihilate your enemy, blow up or capture their base, complete espionage or stealth missions, reach Berlin… Will a videogame's finale ever concern the liberation of Belsen?

Designers of war-themed games have also yet to choose unarmed personnel for their heroes – as if anyone other than a soldier's story is too banal and it's simply inconceivable to imagine playing as a besieged townsperson, as a collaborator, a hostage, someone who shelters declared enemies, a refugee, a medic, a reporter, a disabled veteran, a conscientious objector, a government propagandist, a prison guard, or a gas-chamber engineer.

Nuclear war, meanwhile, renders whole genres of videogame impossible. There's no enemy soldier to shoot against, no battlefield over which to drive your tanks, and no research facility to infiltrate. Even strategy proves unplayable, as the mathematical game theorists of the Cold War period showed. Notoriously, no-one can win an all-out nuclear war. It's a zero-sum game of mutually-assured destruction.

Best not to think, then, of what an actual nuclear conflict might be like to live through. Post-apocalyptic scenarios abound in videogames, dark with dread or gallows humor, but the realities of what actually happened at Hiroshima and Nagasaki in August 1945, the tragedies and heroism of the cities' inhabitants as their world in one instant changed forever, remain absent from videogames.

Your mission, then, is to confront these taboos. Only a few videogames, such as *Peacemaker* and *Balance of Power*, have yet done so with much critical success. Explore how some civilian experiences of war might become the basis of gameplay. Learn what everyday life was actually like in the midst of some historical conflicts – and what it's like right now, for there's almost certainly a war happening somewhere in the world as you read these words. Children find ways to play amongst rubble and carcasses, so how might you, at a safe remove? As a serious games project, learn about peace-building strategies, in theory and practice, and consider how you might present these in the form of a game. Imagine a game being emotionally distressing and unwinnable and yet still playing it out of a feeling of moral compulsion and whatever complex satisfaction (not mere masochism or enjoyment of fear and horror) that can yield.

BOSS FIGHT

Exploring 'violence'

You're unstoppable. Opponents fall before you, one after the other. As your kill-streak mounts – 9, 10, 11 in a row – you unlock ever more powerful weapons. You're becoming like a god, glorious in victory. The fierce joy mounts, welling to your throat as you take on another, and another – how dare he attempt to stop you? Aarrr!!! The roar bursts from the core of your being, uncontainable like the rage of a beast beating its chest and running amok.

Rage is the extreme of anger. Close cousin of righteous indignation, it's a powerful force driving a person to action in response to unbearable affront. It's the emotion that some non-gamers fear videogames actively produce, and not just in a harmless play form.

Recognizing battle as the supreme test of manhood's ability to face or create its destiny, warrior cultures have always awarded highest social honors to their military champions. The so-called martial virtues, named after the Roman god of war, include courage, daring, strength, skill-at-arms, loyalty to country and comrade, love of victory and honor, defiance, and resolve. In ancient Rome, the triumph was a celebratory public procession given to commanders in thanks for their defense of the city or extension of its empire through conquest over other nations. Tribal and national rulers around the world are defined by leading their armies, either in the flesh or symbolically. Norse sagas chose to record, as the jewel of a people's history, the mighty deeds of legendary warriors, for whom awaits a dedicated hall in heaven. For centuries, European literature focused on courtly knights with their code of chivalry. Both Christianity and Islam have concepts of holy war, whose soldiers fight for God. In many religions gods war on demons, or descend to show earthly mortals how it's done, or render a favorite hero invincible.

We do not lack for examples, then, of how to celebrate the spilling of entrails, the splintering of bones, and the splattering of brains in the name of country, god, glory, and a just cause. Awash with their enemies' steaming crimson gore, heroes feel a madness of manly pride and do not come home feeling ashamed. Those military leaders who stand in marble and bronze atop plinths in city squares are celebrated for their necessary use of armed force rather than for their delight in killing. Retrospectively their motivation becomes sanctified by ideas of a larger public good and is washed clean of barbarian blood-lust.

As well as questions about the moral and political necessity of war and law enforcement, we must enter the nature-versus-nurture debate. Part of the function of videogames, as of competitive sports, is arguably to substitute simulated or surrogate violence in place of the real thing. If you believe that aggression and conflict are ineradicable from human nature – or more precisely from what it is to be male – then children's role-play with toy guns, shooter videogames, combat sports, and military service all perform a similar purpose. Namely, they provide a relatively safe outlet for what would otherwise end up in brawls, riots, murder, and war. Young men especially must be allowed to explore and express their testosterone-fuelled competitive urges.

Nonsense, the nurturist replies. All such activities are cultural expressions that *foster* aggression and resort to physical force. Stone-Age men may have had to defend themselves against each other and wild beasts, but why should we suppose they therefore evolved to enjoy and to require regular experiences of killing, rather than to be capable of it in extremity? Gang-related homicides, for example, are the result of social and economic factors, such as unemployment and organized crime, which can at least in principle be changed. Don't encourage the belief that they're somehow an inevitable expression of the power of male hormones.

You're both missing the point, says another. The so-called violence in games is pretend, and not even children confuse it with reality. In fact, argues Gerard Jones in *Killing Monsters: Why Children Need Fantasy, Super Heroes, and Make-Believe Violence*, play violence is psychologically healthy for kids. Parents worry about videogames in the same way they did about waltzing, jazz, and rock 'n' roll, simply because they're expressions of youth culture at the time. People scapegoat videogames to avoid facing up to far more worrying matters, like overly-liberal gun laws, domestic abuse, failing schools, and endemic poverty, to name just a few. All mainstream videogames are carefully age-rated, but many parents appear to ignore this for their own convenience and allow their children to play inappropriate games.

Back and forth, debates about games and 'violence' (which is often ill-defined) contain many more arguments and counter-arguments, evidence and counter-evidence, insult and counter-insult. Bored and frustrated by their repeatedly negative and often stupid portrayal in the media, gamers have grown accustomed to dismissing claims about videogames' potentially harmful effects. *Here we go again.* Yet even if the balance of arguments might be on your side, it's hard to be certain about anything.

Gamers are prevented from further exploring this issue in part because of the hesitation by developers to produce videogames that will offend public opinion and be denied a certificate by the censors (as happened to *Manhunt*). In their explicit and excessive gore, videogames may appear to know few, if any, boundaries. Yet there are some important ways in which games' representation and simulation of violent acts remains cartoonlike and psychologically shallow.

For example, within a game players are largely unable to perform the kind of rituals and expressive acts hunters and soldiers do in the real world. Your character can't pray on the eve of battle, chop off a victim's head for a trophy, or bury the corpse with respect. However hard you try, you can't do anything further to your opponent's body once it's dead. Pump it full of bullets, kick it thirty times, drag and drop it, repeatedly crouch your backside over it, and it'll look just the same. Often it simply vanishes to respawn elsewhere. Endless butchery may be required in order to dispatch aliens, zombies, and fanatics, but within the game this is often a relatively gratuitous necessity, justified by a narrative of individual, national, or species survival but otherwise emptied of personal psychic consequence. Neither gamers nor their avatars commonly feel an urgent need to undergo purification after battle: no need to vomit after killing, no trembling of body or gun.

As yet there are no takers among studios to market the first full-length videogame where you play as a forensic-scientist serial-killer, sadistically obsessed with the minutiae of stalking, kidnapping, torture, rape, murder, cannibalism, postmortem dissection and disposal according to some pathological scheme of sacrifice and salvation. Massively popular in fiction, film, television drama, and documentaries, such grotesque subjects remain too hot for videogames to explore in comparable detail. Readers of a crime novel can read the description of a character joyfully dabbling hands in a victim's gaping wound, and thereby perhaps imagine themselves doing so. Viewers of the same story adapted as a film or stage drama can behold the action more directly with their eyes and ears. But players of a videogame cannot take the further step of performing the simulated action themselves bodily via the game's controls.

Presumably the fear is that physically performing, rather than merely imagining or beholding, acts of simulated violence will have a more corrupting, desensitizing effect on the individual player's moral integrity. In that case, should we not also fear for those small-part actors who perform simulated assaults nightly on Broadway, as extras on movie sets, and as character-actors in true-crime reconstructions, and without whom there would be no bloody dramas, films, or documentaries which it's apparently acceptable for mass audiences to watch?

Socially and ethically, the most important question to ask is, what *is* the best way for us to learn about the real-world causes and consequences of armed conflict and interpersonal violence so that we can minimize these? Part of the answer must lie in exploring the role of news and entertainment media to circulate both fact and fantasy. It's possible that videogames, now or in future, might actually prove to have an inoculatory effect, in other words producing citizens who are *more* likely to be pacifist than non-gamers are. At the moment this seems unlikely, given that a majority of videogames are relentlessly militaristic and focus on producing emotions of fear and triumphalism at spectacles of bodily carnage and physical destruction.

'Nothing in life is to be feared,' wrote the scientist Marie Curie. 'It is only to be understood. Now is the time to understand more, so that we may fear less.' As a relatively new expressive medium, videogames present a fresh opportunity to understand many subjects, including war and violence – artistically, intellectually, and *ludologically*. This is the aim of the following missions. There are plenty of mature, thoughtful players and developers for whom Curie's motto spells out an appropriate level of ambition to hold for at least some videogames, regardless of their dominant function as mainstream commercial entertainment.

Fondle your weapon

Guns, cars, and blades are the primary objects videogames give us with which to exert mastery inside the worlds of play. They've a genre each: shooters, racing games, and hack and slash. Each is a symbol of male power, even though female characters and players can also wield them. Feminists suggest that guns, cars, and blades all stand ultimately for the phallus, that definitive masculine possession. The victory-hungry, alpha-hopeful male waves his around to prove he's more virile than the next man. *Behold my weapon. Kneel before me, for I am king.*

Gun, car, or blade, each is imaginatively loaded with an excess of fantasies that it will somehow transform whoever wields it by enhancing his or her potency. This is the basic principle of a *fetish*, which can be defined as any object, natural or manmade, supposed to possess magical powers. A fetish brings closer those forces that would otherwise lie beyond reach, so they may be at least partly controlled. The vastness of sexual desire, for example, is harnessed into a glove or shoe.

Or we could use the term *glamorization*. In advertising, PR, and showbiz, glamour is the illusion of perfect success possessed by special people whom the rest of us are encouraged to envy. If only I had that car, that body, that house, then I'd be a star and happy too. If only I had that gun, or that knife, then people would respect me...

Yet videogames also show us villains corrupted by too much power, and sometimes the burden of responsibility carried by heroes who reluctantly accept power only in order to fight for good. In reality, most of us don't want too much power or wouldn't know how to use it. On the streets, guns, cars, and blades can destroy lives.

Each has its mythology, deeply embedded in the collective cultural psyche through generations of storytelling and image-making. Their power flows into numerous accessory objects, such as the camera, spaceship, and pen, which extend into both our everyday and fantasy lives. Hollywood scriptwriters could give you a whole catalogue of clichés for guns, cars, and blades: the ultimate world-destroying god-weapon, the most-difficult maneuver only one hero in a generation can pull off, the edge sufficiently sharp to slice the hardest substance, etcetera, etcetera.

With a gun, car, or blade to hand, you don't need muscles – though many a videogame hero will have them too. Each of these tools focuses the general desire for power over others into a singular object. It's then possible for small and slender heroes, male or female, to loom over their larger rivals by virtue of the metal in their hand. They've both the means and the mental toughness to use it so as to force bigger opponents to submit.

Today cars are rarely advertised via bikini-clad women draped across shiny bonnets. The image remains a provocative metaphor, however, for male appetite for fast cars. After all, what else can women do in the world of racing, apparently, except arouse men to compete? In this case, as with guns and blades, erotic charge seems to derive from the possibly fatal contact between warm, tender, yielding flesh and cold, hard, brutal metal.

Mario's racing karts, by contrast, are cuddly and wouldn't hurt anyone. Pop-guns make shooting comical. Children play with wooden or plastic swords. Videogames, like other forms of popular culture, take special care that 'real' weapons should never enter such innocent worlds. When *American McGee's Alice* puts a kitchen knife in Alice's hand, Wonderland is turned into a place of bloody horror no longer suitable, according to the rating certificate, for even young teenagers.

In many videogames guns, cars, and blades come ready-fetishized, sometimes laughably so. An artist has sculpted the phallic shape, a 3D-modeler has polished the metal, and an animator choreographed the hero to stand with legs astride and clutching in both hands the massive tool rising from hip or groin. There's rarely anything you can do to change this, even if you can holster your gun, vacate the car, and drop your blade.

In particular games, how do the designers glamorize these objects and exaggerate the power they bestow on their owner? Or by contrast make them bent, grubby, and unheroic?

What thrill, if any, do you get from wielding these weapons in the imaginary worlds of particular videogames? What storyline unfolds, or what spectacular actions do you get to perform using them? How does a gun, a car, or a blade invite you to feel more powerful and sexy, and to what extent do you accept this invitation? Are you attracted or repulsed, filled with desire or with fear?

Are you drawn more by guns, by cars, or by blades? What is it that excites or revolts you in this weapon's form, function, and mythology?

Defeat your symbolic father

Videogames abound in scenarios where the player-character defeats a male figure of power and authority. They stage this archetypal conflict again and again – because it's a sure-fire way of hooking you in emotionally, because our culture is in some way built around it. New York godfather, wicked Arabian vizier, dark master-magician, orc king, mad scientist, evil turtle, alien commander, or renegade ex-KGB general: who else are these bosses than symbolic father figures?

Just consider how often the boss, whether in a videogame, action movie, school, or workplace, is in fact an older or rival male. *If these bosses were to symbolize the members of your family, who else could they be than your father, or an elder brother, uncle, or stepfather seeking to take his place as head of the family?* And *if* your emotions towards your father (brother, uncle, stepfather) are at all powerful, why wouldn't they find expression wherever you meet similar figures in the rest of your life, whether in the classroom or in a game?

Or look at it another way. Where does the emotion come from that makes a player *want* to defeat the boss so badly, especially when there are no other players present to show off to? The boss taunts the player and despises his or her weaknesses and failings. The last time you wanted to prove yourself that badly was when you were a small child pitched against your father or elder brother's adult might.

History and art tell many stories of sons impatient to replace their father as head of the empire. A prince murders the king to gain the throne, an ambitious business graduate pushes to take over the family firm, a teenage son verbally and then physically challenges his father in the home. *Hurry up and move aside, old man, it's my turn already. Let me start spending the money, doing as I please, running the show*. In this scenario, the villain is often a precocious upstart crazed by perceived parental oppression, or else driven through long suffering to break the Commandment, honor thy father... Whether you grew up with a father you loved, a father you hated, or no father at all, there'd be no need for a Commandment if the relationship between one generation and the next (as between humankind, its earthly leaders, and heavenly powers) wasn't *always* fraught in some way or another.

Fictional stories of conflict between father and son enable us to experience emotions and follow impulses that are forbidden in real life. Their symbolic function is similar to that of dreams, which speak with the shocking, uncensored voice of our unconscious.

A key thinker here, albeit with a deservedly problematic reputation, is Sigmund Freud. His most widely-popularized theories concern the unconscious mind and repressed sexual desires, especially those originating during childhood. Every child, he suggests, goes through a process of adjustment as it comes to terms with its primary relationships with its parents, which reflect the constraints on behavior required to live in society. This process normally produces certain fantasies, anxieties, and conflicts, which persist into the adult's psychological makeup, mostly at a subconscious level. Some individuals become so psychologically mixed up, either by their parents or by the constraints of society, that breakdown and the need for psychotherapeutic treatment become inevitable.

One of Freud's major models for the child-parent relationship is the Oedipus Complex, named after a character in Ancient Greek mythology who accidentally (!) kills his father, who is King of Thebes, and sleeps with his mother. Freud takes this shocker and applies it to infant psychology by proposing that a boy-child's desire to monopolize his mother's attention leads to envy of his father. The myth of Oedipus presents this conflict in an extreme form by identifying its root emotions as something comparable to sexual desire and murderous hatred. Most children resolve the Oedipal conflict, in the case of a boy by identifying with his father. Those who fail to resolve the conflict carry it into their adult sexuality, for example by desiring partners who closely resemble one of their parents.

These are only the bare bones of the theory. Unsurprisingly it's proven controversial, especially when taken too literally. Freud uses the Oedipal story more or less metaphorically to help understand some of the conflicting emotions which might occur, unformulated, in a child's mind as its grows up.

Focused on a male child in a nuclear family, the Oedipus Complex seems ill-suited to explaining the dynamics of other common types of family, such as with a single parent or girl child. What happens, then, if you're a female gamer fighting a male boss, which is what many videogames ask you to do? Must you pretend to be a man in a man's world? Or does the boss somehow become your symbolic mother in male drag? If more women designed games, would we predict them to present mostly scenarios where the heroine kills an older woman in a mirror image of the Oedipal story?

You might be tempted to dismiss these as academic, not real questions at all. Can't an orc king be just an orc king, for once, and not a father-in-disguise? This kind of response, while understandable, will struggle to explain why gamers do sometimes appear to identify in depth with the characters and roles they play. Can you truthfully say your passion for videogames is always a wholly straightforward pleasure, entirely separated off from any other aspect of your psychology?

Notice what parent-child roles occur in particular videogames and how they're aligned with male, female, or other gender. Unless the game is quite abstract, such as a puzzle, assume that family relationships are potentially always present in some form, in so far as these are inescapably part of you, the game's designers, and all human cultures. Sometimes family archetypes will be explicit, as when humanoid characters are portrayed as parental figures. On other occasions you might feel more like an abandoned child in search of a parent or siblings and finding only the symbolic substitutes of strangers and aliens. In either case, how can you understand your personal emotional involvement with the game, including your need to win it, in terms of family relationships, intergenerational conflicts, and the struggle for male power? How might the game also invite you to take on a parental role yourself, and what complications does that bring? Or how, on the contrary, do videogames pretend to help you escape the whole messy business of family relationships altogether?

Query biceps and breasts

There aren't enough hours in the day to devote yourself to both your console and the gym. Luckily you've no need to break sweat since you can play as a character who's already pumped iron and tread-milled the miles for you. Numerous videogame heroes parade their bulging biceps and beefy torsos. Hyper-sexualized female characters are notoriously top-heavy and wasp-waisted. Rare is the gamer whose body remotely resembles either of these idealized physiques.

In action-adventure and fighting games, the characters' athleticism can be explained by what they do, so there's a degree of realism. What's not explained is that enormous bust, nor the freakish girth of macho arms, necks, and thighs that surely come only from steroids. These bodies are at least half fantasy.

Similar bodies appear in Hollywood movies, fashion advertising, music videos, and elsewhere in popular culture. Together they seek to persuade us to a broad acceptance of muscular men and large-breasted, thin-waisted women as models of sexual attractiveness. Like a sports car confined to low gears on public roads, such perfected bodies have no practical purpose in modern life. According to evolutionary biologists, we're hardwired to admire visible signs of physical health and vitality, such as a generally fit physique and clear complexion, as indications that a potential partner could help us to produce healthy offspring. You don't need a fashion-model or movie-star body to pass this test, though.

As *flesh*, biceps and breasts serve essential bodily functions. As *images*, however, they communicate a range of social and cultural meanings, clustered around the idea of sexual potency and status among peers. At a nightclub or in a dating-agency profile, how a person chooses to bare some flesh can be interpreted as indicating their sexual availability and proficiency. From fashion images, young people of both sexes learn a variety of poses that emphasize their assets so as to present a tough-guy or sultry-chick persona.

While none of the above are original insights, body-image remains an important aspect of contemporary culture, partly because its power is renewed with each generation of young men and women.

The meanings read into an individual's body aren't always under his or her control. Thus in different situations the bulge of a guy's biceps might be interpreted as a sign of stupidity, vanity, brutality, sportiness, or homosexuality, depending on the social context or assumptions made by the viewer. Artists who design commercial videogame characters do aim to control the meanings communicated by selected body images. On box-cover art especially, with its heightened visual glamour, artists send messages about the hero's personality and how players should feel about him or her. Lead characters always pose, telling us their attitude towards events within the game and by implication to the wider world of real life. Whether bare-fleshed, armored, or clothed, whether human, alien, or part-machine, videogame characters' bodies are typically powerful and draw in some way on fantasies of the perfect male or female physique.

The artists' knowledge, whether conscious or not, comes from exposure to all those other images in the culture that also draw on these fantasies. That's exactly how the player, too, comes to be able to read the cover image. Time after time you've learnt what an action hero or fashion model looks like, without anyone needing to explain this to you.

How to *analyze* fashion images – among which we can count videogame box-cover art – is a different kind of skill, however (academically called semiotics). It's quite easy to start. Basically, you identify the various parts of the image that convey meanings to the viewer. Lara Croft's trademark boots, for example, have been chosen by the artist from all the other kinds of footwear she could wear. Her character would be very different in flip-flops or stilettos, say. Her particular style of side-buckled, mid-calf, leather boots, varying slightly across games and terrains, tells us she's an outdoor action girl, ready to kick and clamber like the toughest marine, and making no concessions to supposed feminine weakness – whether in a fight or in the bedroom. You can analyze the rest of her outfit in a similar way. Everything she wears may have a practical explanation, themed around army and expedition clothing, but everything is sexualized, too. Each item has a straightforward meaning (denotation) but also layers of associated meaning (connotation) – what's meant along with the primary meaning, implied rather than stated explicitly.

It's through these implied, associated meanings that images such as Lara Croft's boots, as much as her breasts, invite players to feel sexy. This isn't simply a matter of wanting to possess her or to be her. We're not pleased *for* Lara that she's lucky to have such a body. Her image, along with countless others both female and male, instead enables us to feel we too are in some way connected to a source of unbounded vigorous energy. They affirm the existence of an ocean of urgent vitality that can be expressed sexually or in physical action such as combat.

Analyzing media images in this way is difficult for several reasons. Implied meanings seem so subjective and ambiguous. Personally we may be reluctant to admit that images might have real power over us even if we do see through them, or that we have an emotional investment in the larger cultural fantasies, such as that of the busty babe and muscle man, that generate particular images. We laugh at them as if to prove we're immune, even if other people aren't. Finally, we're unused to articulating in detail how an image may arouse us by appealing to our gaze.

Yet opportunities to practice this kind of analysis lie all around us, if we're sufficiently motivated to stop and think. Biceps and breasts will not disappear from box-cover art any time soon, because the symbolic power they hold is too important and too easy for developers to exploit.

Trace the Hero's Journey

Defeat the forces of evil, conquer the world, rescue the princess, attain the peak of power, revenge a great wrong, protect the innocent, solve the crime, explore the unknown, fulfill your destiny... Videogames invite us again and again to take the role of hero. His, or occasionally her, journey takes many forms and passes through many different worlds. Its structure, though, usually follows the same basic course. Game writers (also called narrative designers) know this as the Hero's Journey.

This term derives from the work of mythology scholars, particularly Joseph Campbell, who compared stories from different cultures around the world as these became available for study following the period of imperial expansion and global trade in the nineteenth century. What they discovered was that certain basic patterns of storytelling appear to be shared across all human societies, from Kurds to Maoris, from Christians to Hindus, from Classical Greece to modern Britain. Examine a Russian folktale, the ghetto-to-Beverly Hills story of an American rap star, and the life of Buddha, and even in such apparently disconnected examples of culture you'll find elements of a common way of shaping the meaning of human experience. Campbell calls this the 'monomyth,' though it's debatable whether it's as singular and universal as this term implies.

In outline it's as follows.

We find our hero in the ordinary world – whatever that is for the particular story. From this hitherto normal existence, whether high or low in his society, the hero is called to undertake an adventure that leads him into an unknown world beyond. Willingly or not, he must leave home and set out upon the road.

There he meets friends and foes, menaces and marvels. In order to proceed he must pass tests and overcome obstacles, including a near-death ordeal that utterly transforms his perceptions. Along the way, every major character the hero meets serves an archetypal purpose.

Among these, a mentor teaches and guides him, a guardian forbids him to pass, an initiatrix (powerful female force) challenges him about the meaning of existence, a shape-shifter appears in various guises, tricksters create mischief and provide comic relief, allies offer moral and team-support, and shadows confront the hero with his greatest fears and tempt him through his greatest weaknesses.

After many trials, the hero achieves his goal. Now, bearing a powerful gift, he must return to his people. This may prove difficult, and at the last moment he could lose everything. Finally he reaches home. Sometimes he receives a hero's welcome. Sometimes it's no longer a place where he can live, so that he soon departs, back into the world beyond.

Thanks to its popularization by Christopher Vogler's *The Writer's Journey*, Hollywood scriptwriters know this pattern inside-out. It's one of their basic formulae. *Star Wars*, *The Wizard of Oz*, and *The Lord of the Rings* trilogy all illustrate the Hero's Journey nicely, as do countless more pedestrian movies.

Once you start looking, you'll find that many videogames use elements of the Hero's Journey to shape their story. Often the easiest things to spot are key turning points in the story and the archetypal role played by each of the main characters. Bear in mind that not all the elements need to appear and not necessarily in the precise order outlined above. Elements can be represented by seemingly trivial and unlikely things or exaggerated into an unmissable spectacle.

Notice how everything is oriented around the player-hero. He or she keeps occupying center-stage as if the whole world revolves around this person. The camera literally follows their every move – it seems too obvious to say. In moments of tension, the music swells to make you feel more heroic. Often there's a proud theme-tune with full orchestra and strong use of brass instruments, which plays as the game loads or at idle moments to remind the player of the destiny awaiting. After a while it may go quiet or shift into a minor key to evoke the lulls before and after a major effort or the pathos of loss and hardship along the way.

You'll find that in most videogames the bulk of play consists of the tests-and-obstacles phase. Often the 'call to adventure' is compressed into an opening cinematic sequence. In fact many videogames cast the player as a permanent adventurer, who left home long ago and whose whole life now happens on the road. There's no retirement or happy family at the end of the game, partly because the game's developers have a commercial incentive to create a franchise of one game after the other featuring the same hero.

This truncation of the Hero's Journey helps explain why some critics perceive videogames to be an adolescent medium that refuses to grow up. One version of the Journey is a traditional initiation ceremony, designed to enable a young person's passage into adulthood. The young person must set out, but they must also complete the return to take their rightful place in society. On the other hand, the Journey is always an idealized representation of an exemplary life, which only exceptional humans – such as the great religious teachers – complete absolutely. The rest of us embark upon the Journey again and again throughout our lives, in different ways and focusing on different phases of the cycle. A culture's myths and stories likewise keep returning to the ideal of heroism, re-expressing it for each new generation.

Heroes come in many flavors. Antiheroes do many bad things and should be villains, but possess some redeeming quality that wins our affection or admiration. Reluctant and accidental heroes are thrust into adventure against their will or unprepared. The efforts and achievements of unsung heroes go unrecognized. Sacrificial heroes are prepared to die for a good cause. The adventures of everyday heroes – some would say the most important of all – take place in the ordinary worlds of work, home, and neighborhood. Those of romantic heroes revolve around the bedroom. Those of mock heroes occupy a miniature scale and make us laugh, whereas the self-destruction of tragic heroes, whose otherwise noble character is spoiled by a single flaw, is grueling to behold. National heroes are usually political leaders or outstanding military personnel. They especially illustrate that one country or tribe's hero may be another's criminal.

In answer to the question What is a hero? you're probably drawn to one kind more than another. Heroes function as role-models. They can inspire us to go beyond what we, or those around us, normally consider to be the limitations of our capability. This isn't automatically for the better. Who are your videogame heroes, and for what values do they stand? Do they enable you to practice being a hero in real life? Or do heroes belong only in the land of make-believe?

Relive your greatest victory or defeat

Winning and losing are so central to videogames that many players have memories of pivotal moments in their personal history when the desire for victory was gloriously fulfilled or cruelly dashed. What's been your supreme triumph as a gamer, or your worst humiliation? Your mission is simply to recall the circumstances, emotions, and killer blows of a pivotal experience, preferably player versus player, either online or face-to-face, and perhaps with an audience of other players to witness your pride or shame.

Various experiences may come to mind. *Any* victory or defeat will do that produced some degree of emotional ferment inside you. Perhaps your heart beats faster just to think of it, or a hot blush rises to your cheeks. Each victory and defeat echoes the emotions generated by previous experiences, including any especially powerful ones which might have occurred during the formative years of youth and childhood. Such moments, taken together, have shaped your destiny as a player and helped make you what you are today.

Relive the victory or defeat as vividly as you can. What's important is to describe the events and feelings *in the present tense* and as if they're happening to you *in reality*, not just as images on a screen: I'm down to my last bullet, I can almost see the look of terror in his eyes... This will help to bring the whole experience alive. Enter into some of the details – the who, what, when, how, and why – as if they're unfolding right now around you.

In truth the moment is not yet over. On some level you're still smiling over the sweet taste of triumph, or grimacing at the bitterness of humiliation, which continue in small ways to color your outlook on life. How does winning or losing matter to you? What dance of pleasure and pain do you perform over the years by being competitive? Do you hope one day to 'win' at real life? Surely this can never be as clear-cut as in a game; every success has its price, every failure has its unexpected benefit, and sometimes it's difficult to tell which is which.

Even in our most seemingly unique, formative experiences we're never alone, never outside the collective history of humanity. From ancient myth and holy texts to Shakespearean drama, Hollywood movies, and tomorrow's videogames, the various stories of the Warrior's Way constitute truths of human experience throughout the ages, as captured in a stream of clichés of contest, victory, and defeat. Which of these do you recognize as naming your personal experience?

Achilles' heel (fatal weakness), bookie's favorite, long-shot, beginner's luck, brains versus brawn, David and Goliath, people's champion, underdog, mystery (masked) contender, the king is dead long live the king, comeback kid, out of retirement, one last fight, discretion is the better half of valor, live to fight another day, strategic retreat, run for your life, tail between your legs, retire to lick your wounds, duel, winner takes all, honorable draw, endgame, fight to the death, no prisoners, no surrender, last stand (Thermopylae), fight to the last man, force of nature, wipe the floor with them, cat playing with a mouse, lesson from the master, putting upstarts in their place, crushing defeat, here comes the cavalry, snatched from the jaws of death, saved at the eleventh hour, hollow (Pyrrhic) victory, lose the battle but win the war, heroic failure, moral victory, kick a man when he's down, stabbed in the back, no holds barred, playing dirty, all's fair in love and war, no-win scenario, zero-sum game, mutually assured destruction, old rivals, derby match, return match, revenge is sweet or a dish best served cold, pride comes before a fall, famous last words, tall story, fisherman's tale (there were *this* many), valley of death, ambush and massacre, bloodbath, killing frenzy, going berserk, blood-lust, war of attrition, standoff, stalemate, deadlock, impasse broken by a stroke of luck, cunning ploy, noble sacrifice, or betrayal…

Contemplate your in-game deaths

In videogames it's common to die over and over until you beat the game or give up. Your character falls to her death with a faintly erotic sigh or explodes into colorful coins and then cheerfully reforms. You're evicted from first-person viewpoint and watch your character lose limbs, spurt blood, and fold to the floor like a slow-motion car-crash test-dummy. To die is nothing, or spectacular at first then increasingly frustrating as you're denied progress, and passing finally into boredom. Resurrection mostly comes cheap, and often you're simply returned back where you left off so that you might just as well have rewound, as the Prince of Persia does with the help of his magical dagger in *The Sands of Time*.

Each episode of the television drama series, *Six Feet Under*, set in a Californian funeral home, starts by showing the death of someone soon to arrive on the embalming table. The scriptwriters' invention of ways to die, often in bizarre accidents that defy the viewer's guesswork, is one of the delights of the show. Most videogames, by contrast, necessarily limit how characters die by rules of play and display: your health bar empties under repeated hits and your character drops elegantly to the ground, for example. Like the staggering of melodramatic heroines from stage-left to stage-right, or the darkness enfolding the eyes of Homer's be-speared heroes on the fields of Troy in *The Iliad*, death-throes in videogames are formulaic.

There are also complex, subtle, and disturbing ways for our characters to die, and us with them vicariously. Horror games especially steep us in an atmosphere of dreadful fatality. As in life, though, we may be too busy to stop and contemplate the mortality of our avatars. Many games provide us with constant stimulation to try again, seek success, keep exploring. No sooner does the controller hang idle in our hands than the game starts playing teaser cinematics or the avatar fidgets, tempting us to resume. There's no such thing as a decent period of mourning after our character has been shot in the head or fallen from a high tower. Nor does our character experience mental trauma or religious conversion as a result of their dip into the abyss. Returned to play, they do not hold life more precious; their faith is neither shaken nor stirred.

'I want to cry every time when Aeris dies,' says a fan of the classic Japanese role-playing game, *Final Fantasy VII*. Making us care that much about characters is a Holy Grail of game design. Major playable characters rarely die during a game's story, for obvious reasons. Firstly, we're typically cast as a hero destined to defeat every enemy and survive every peril no-matter how seemingly fatal. Secondly, killing off our character as part of the game's story must stop us from playing – unless we're to follow him or her into an afterlife or switch to playing another character, which would be such significant shifts in the story as to require working into the game's whole premise.

Along with love, death is one of the great themes of art and philosophy throughout the ages. It's the stuff of comedy as much as tragedy.

a. Simply notice what happens the next time you die in a game. And when you die again. And again. Which games that you've played occur to you to confirm or challenge the general description given above? Recall and explore what moved, intrigued, or frustrated you in the way the game handled death.

b. Many games present the imminent approach of the hero's death-in-combat as an audiovisual treat, with blood-spatters on the display and the sounds of laboring breath and heartbeat. How might a videogame explore the more ordinary experiences of dying that occur to the majority of humanity? Here lie mystery, emotional power, and opportunity for creative invention. Start to imagine what it might be like to *play* the experience of lying on your deathbed. To some extent this is what people have always done, though it's not usually named as such: fighting to stay alive, navigating the maze of a lifetime's memories, securing religious salvation, outwitting vulturous relatives, making peace with loved ones…

c. You've read this far, so the thought of death presumably doesn't utterly terrify you. Assuming you're not already, become for a while thoroughly *morbid* about videogames. Develop a fascination with how they handle death and how you may approach your own inevitable mortality through the experience of playing. Some people regard such a fascination as dangerous and unhealthy. Are you persuaded by black-clad existentialists and Goths, that confronting the fact of death is a necessary step in becoming a more mature and authentic individual? Maybe playing videogames can then remind us of our mortality and teach us how to live with that knowledge – unless they're devoted to helping us ignore the one certainty of life.

Play to lose

The only kind of Chess I liked as a teenager was Loser's, also known as Anti or Suicide. Pieces move as in usual Chess, but capturing is compulsory and the winner is the first person to lose all their pieces. Ordinary Chess, with its careful deliberations, merely confronted me with my mental shortcomings. Loser's Chess, with its common feature of long sequences of forced capture, provided an extravagant spectacle of massacred troops – much more fun.

Card games such as Bluff (Cheat) and puzzles games like *Tetris* work on a similar principle whereby play focuses on shedding rather than collecting, on loss rather than acquisition. Pieces turn into a burden or contamination. Your largest, most valuable or powerful piece becomes your greatest liability. An established direction of play is thus reversed, which is a novelty in itself providing pleasure.

The aim of Loser's Chess is still to win the game, just according to revised rules. In this sense it's not really a game for losers at all. Players can be as competitive and strategic as in ordinary Chess. Yet not winning at Loser's Chess didn't matter so much for me, since the massacre of pieces and the disruption of rules, whoever won, felt like some kind of moral victory in themselves.

Some political games and in-game protests position players so it's impossible to win, or winning doesn't feel good like it should. In *New York Defender*, the player attempts to shoot down planes aiming to crash into the Twin Towers. As in *Space Invaders*, the player is doomed to fail sooner or later. Whereas the arcade classic is fun to play despite this inevitability, *New York Defender*, in part because of the real-world pain associated with the events of 9/11, is not much fun at all. In his *dead-in-iraq* project, Joseph DeLappe logs into the U.S. Army's official recruitment game, *America's Army*, a massively popular online shooter, in order to type out the names of actual U.S. soldiers who've been killed during the ongoing conflict in Iraq. The other players logged in are intent on simulating combat missions, and many of them don't like anyone interrupting their fun.

According to common wisdom, there's nothing so annoying as a spoilsport who won't 'play properly' because they've no chance of winning. The unspoken rule is: don't play if you can't respect the game. Playing to lose is simply rude, and nobody likes a bad loser. Similarly, designers have no business creating games that mock the player's legitimate desire to have fun and to win. So dominant is this assumption that in many games it's literally impossible to play to lose. The game simply comes to a halt or dead-end if you fail to progress or compete in more or less the anticipated manner.

An enduring motif in militaristic narratives, also present in myths and religions worldwide, is the sacrificial death. A hero nobly gives himself up for the greater good. The forces of evil gleefully take his life without realizing they thereby seal their own ultimate defeat. Passive resistance extends this principle from a one-off, individual event to an ongoing, collective process. Short-term loss is revealed as long-term victory. Provided the storyline does deliver this payoff, even the most painful sacrifice can be borne, whether in videogames or other media. Sacrifices that are shown to be misguided or in vain, however, insult our sense of justice and are therefore unpopular. Not just as individuals but as larger social groups, whole nations, and as a species we like to believe we're on the winning side, if not in the present then at least in the long run of history and eternity.

a. In which videogames would it be possible and interesting to sabotage play by refusing to follow the rules for trying to win? Note that this is different from cheating in order to win. What would be the point of your protest? What larger victory could you aim to achieve through your sacrifice? If you go on to implement your experiment, how do other players actually respond when they realize you're playing to lose?

b. Choose a type of videogame you enjoy and consider how you could rewrite its rules so that, in order to win, the player would need to do the opposite of what they would usually do. Competition would then revolve around achieving this action. For example, in a loser's racing game the winner is the *last* person to cross the finishing line, and in a loser's beat-'em-up the aim is to be the *first* one knocked out. In each case, your task it to reorient the gameplay so as to create an interesting set of challenges.

Feel the blows

Your character is taking a pounding. You fight back, giving as good as you get. They come at you again, raining punches upon your body. A high kick catches you under the chin, you're lifted in a graceful arc through the air and crumple to the ground. Or the crowbar they're wielding crunches into your shoulder, and your knees fold beneath you. A moment later you spring back to your feet. You must be made of steel, endorphins pump through your brain, for you shake off the pain and attack once more with undiminished vigor.

The cartoon fisticuffs of beat-'em-ups and melee fights happens so fast, even in the cinematic replay that follows each knockout, that you've little chance to examine individual blows. Slow-motion, frame-by-frame replay of a recording is required.

In some ways the physicality of the fight does appear in detail. Bursts of color explode at the site of impact, and in some games gobs of blood spurt and shower liberally. To listen, it's all grunts and roars, shrieks and yells. Yet all this remains fantastic. No-one that matters is seriously hurt. Knocked out one moment, they're back on their feet, good as new, the next. Like the agony of wrestlers, taking turns in bringing each other to the brink of submission, it's a performance staged for family entertainment. Good, wholesome fun. No bones or spines are broken, no organs ruptured or brains damaged, no bodies ruined for life. Instead it's a melodrama, whether of champions sparring for a title, good fighting evil, or superheroes versus mutants.

The trading of blows is acted out so that even those in the back row can see. 'Ouch, that's gotta hurt.' A grimace momentarily stretches from ear to ear, the sufferer briefly staggers, or howls, or shakes his head in disbelief. Yet all this remains an external image only. We don't feel anything inside our own bodies that corresponds to what the sufferer must be feeling. Their pain, if it's real at all, remains out of our imaginative reach, something we cannot share in sympathy. If anything, someone else's pain during combat feels *sweet* to us by satisfying our desire for a compelling drama of suffering and endurance, victory and humiliation.

There are numerous variations on this basic scenario. Fighting has its own genre and also occurs across many different types of videogame, including wrestling and boxing simulations, punch-ups in action-adventure games, plus combat using close-range weapons. Storylines vary as well as degrees of realism in representation. Some games requiring violence against realistic human opponents, such as identical guards or thugs, enable the player to conveniently knock or smother someone into unconsciousness to avoid killing or even paining them. Mature-certificate games, by contrast, feature violence intended to be more horrific and graphic, though not yet what might be called torture porn.

Some games have ways to show the player that their character is experiencing pain and weakness as a result of injuries, poison, and so forth. This is usually generalized rather than attached to a specific wound. The screen image begins to blur or turns red, but you can't look down and inspect the gaping hole in your side, nor press buttons on the controller to staunch the wound or apply a bandage. These things are done automatically or conveniently forgotten. Walk into a medical kit or swallow a green pill and the wounds and radiation sickness magically heal. This is all part of the *lack* of realism that makes videogames fun to play.

In our physical bodies most of us hope never to be hit, or at least not in anger. The meaning of a blow depends on its context. In play-fighting, children develop strength, endurance, and social skills by exerting and being on the receiving end of physical force. Many people enjoy contact sports, such as martial arts, which can be intensely competitive. Masochists reputedly obtain sexual satisfaction from being subjected to pain, within certain limits. Hooligans may look forward to Saturday night's brawl. For their participants, these activities do not constitute 'violence' as they might appear to for onlookers. Within each context, blows are more or less willingly exchanged as the means of participation in a rewarding social activity. Pain is the price paid for whatever pleasure is gained.

This is presumably how gamers feel about that other, less visible but more literal form of violence in videogaming. We feel the blows through sore eyes, repetitive strain injury, headaches, and nervous tics. Gaming is a physical activity, even though most of the time players remain sitting, far less active than their counterparts who whirl and clamber onscreen. Gaming impacts on the body, famously through the thumbs. Occasionally this fact reaches the headlines, but mostly it's an untold story about which console manufacturers, game developers, and reviewers remain understandably reticent. Yet videogames aren't much different from other activities in this respect. Learn to touch-type or play the guitar and you'll notice the physical impact on your body as it adjusts, with aches taking root in your wrists and calluses hardening on your fingertips.

a. Take time to acknowledge some physical symptoms of your gaming life, especially when you overdo it. Direct your awareness, if you can, to what that part of your body feels like during and after play.

b. Choose one or two in-game blows delivered by or to your character and try to imagine what it would feel like to receive yourself physically. Is the object delivering the blow blunt or sharp? Which precise part of your body does it make contact with? What damage does it cause as it enters and to which of your tissues – muscle, bone, vein, skin, or organ? Visualize the nerves to these tissues screaming so that nothing exists for the victim (you) except agony.

c. Research to learn from a medical perspective what actually happens to a human body when it's punctured, beaten, or wrenched. Recognize the chasm between this reality and the spectacular presentation of cartoon brawls.

With your expanded medical knowledge, imagine how a videogame might show more of the detail of wounding. How might it also make playable more of the inner experience of enduring pain? How engrossing would a game have to be in order for this to still be part of having 'fun'?

EPISODE 2: THE INNERMOST CAVE

Gnōthi sauton (know thyself)

Why study videogames? As a relatively new, youth-oriented medium, videogames have yet to be recognized in many institutions as a 'proper subject' worthy of study. Traditionalists are unlikely to change their opinion about this any time soon, despite videogames' self-evident influence as both a major global entertainment industry and an emerging electronic art-form. Yet for many current teenagers and twenty-somethings, gaming is such a cornerstone of their media experience that the idea videogames should be singled out for *exclusion* from study is perverse.

Once you trouble to look, there's a lot to understand, including games' technology and production, their psychological and social functions, their narrative and artistic qualities, and educative value. Videogames provoke ongoing public debates and controversies which deserve well-informed contributions, not kneejerk reactions. By studying videogames we may hope to improve their criticism and thereby help to encourage the development of 'better' games – indeed, to understand what that might mean.

What mirror can videogames hold up to society and to individuals?

How do videogames enhance or diminish our abilities to make meaning?

How do they engage us with 'reality' as well as help us to escape it?

How might videogames liberate or enslave, civilize or barbarize?

What ambitions might we have for this medium in the future?

These are some of the questions that might drive our study of videogames, a study that should entail both appreciation and criticism. Among other things, criticism should at times go against the grain of gaming's predominantly consumerist culture, which tends to discourage too much, or at least certain kinds of, thinking. When someone buys a videogame, this transaction is often a simple commercial one, in which a stated sum of money supposedly secures a certain portion of entertainment. In-store there's no assistant helping customers to question the advertising promise and ask whether they can reasonably expect their purchase to meet any deeper needs, such as for a lasting sense of self-worth. That would be absurd. Even personal shopping advisers are not life counselors.

Games are designed to deliver the player some very obvious kinds of pleasure, mostly of the lighthearted and ephemeral kind. With the exception of so-called serious (educational or political) games, they're supposed above all to be 'fun.' Few videogames aim to improve the player socially, morally, or intellectually, though arguably many of them do perform this function in their own way. Like other forms of popular entertainment, their primary business is to amuse and provide a holiday from work, politics, and other troubles. They're created with this purpose in mind. Basic questions to ask about games therefore center on how and why they're fun to play.

Why is one game more appealing than another?

How do videogames compare to other forms of popular entertainment?

What motivates the individual player to keep playing?

When are the pleasures of particular games innocent and when might they be harmful?

The pleasures of gaming are examples of what philosophers call *aesthetics*. Naming videogames in this way places them alongside older art-forms. They sit there uncomfortably, like a schoolboy fidgeting to run into the playground. Yet players may appreciate beauty, originality, skill, and expressive power in videogames just as much as spectators enjoying more traditional art-forms, such as music, drama, poetry, and architecture. Ingenuity and elegance of design, enchantments of a well-told story, delighting of eye and ear, rhythmic movement, and communal appreciation – such are the basic aesthetic pleasures offered with varying emphasis by *all* the creative arts humans have ever invented, videogames included.

Designers, critics, and academics have begun to spell out how videogames deliver these experiences in ways specific to the medium. Crucially, videogames require explicit physical participation via the controls. Players enjoy performing actions within the game and feeling that these directly contribute to the game's outcome.

According to some commonly-accepted principles of effective game design, the player is most likely to enjoy a game when he or she progresses through a structured sequence of challenges that produces a repetitive pattern of failure leading to success. The designer aims to steer the player between the rocks of boredom and frustration: neither too easy nor too difficult, neither too samey nor too varied. The player swaggers out confidently and is knocked down, picks herself up and tries again, eventually achieves some degree of mastery. This process occurs in a make-believe play-world set aside from ordinary life – the so-called magic circle – where the rules of the game artificially constrain what you can do and thereby enable you to win, whether one point or many.

Videogames use a technological, audiovisual medium that's intended to be pleasurable in its own right, though ugly and ear-jarring games do exist, and even latest-generation consoles are liable to crash. The player develops motor skills in the use of the controls, whether on a keyboard or other device. Games' demand for coordinated response and increasing fluency with these controls can be a major source of satisfaction in its own right.

Some observers have characterized the whole experience as a form of learning made pleasurable by being detached from formal educational settings and real-world consequences.

Game designers and academics may be experts in these matters, but their expertise generally runs out before reaching answers to larger questions concerning the contribution videogames make to players' overall happiness. As entertainment products, games' stated aim is to contribute in small or major ways to the joys of life. Yet love, fulfillment, and well-being are perennial imponderables. Hedonic psychology, the contemporary study of what, in practice, actually makes people happy, has roots in ancient Greek philosophy. It offers many intriguing insights into gaming pleasure, such as the idea of 'flow' that's become popular across a variety of youth subcultures.

One of the Greek philosophers' central concerns is summed up in the phrase *gnōthi sauton*, translated as *know thyself*. Arguably the ultimate reason for studying videogames – or anything at all – is to understand who we are: something possible only by studying how we experience and interact with the worlds around and within us. This is the focus of the missions in this section.

Several factors discourage gamers from being more thoughtful about their pastime. These factors are powerful, so that you are an exception among gamers in having read this far.

Gamers are not renowned for philosophical introspection, nor for political activism. The serious games movement is largely detached from the commercial mainstream of videogame production. When someone describes themselves as an 'avid gamer' this term stereotypically connotes near-obsessive playing sessions and participation in gamer culture at the expense of broader social participation and greater self-knowledge. On occasions, gaming can be a myopic and ghettoized pursuit.

Games have rather a bad reputation among non-gamers which it's potentially a bore to have to counter. From personal experience as a player, you may be certain this reputation is based on misunderstanding. Still, do you have the patience and love of debate required to correct this error, again and again, with well-informed and persuasive argument rather than stock responses of denial and derision? Where are the glories to be won from defending videogames against their detractors compared to the more immediate triumphs available simply by playing and succeeding in whatever's your current favorite game?

As a relatively new entertainment medium, videogames don't yet have a body of socially-respected advocates, such as well-known critics and named designers. Who else will raise the standards of wider public debate and speak for videogames against cross-cultural, comparative standards? For every hundred reviewers who can score a videogame out of ten, how many are competent to explain its merits to intelligent, culturally-literate non-gamers?

Much of the 'coolness' of videogames consists precisely in their incomprehensibility to older generations. Why should younger gamers scrutinize this medium if they assume it represents an advanced future continuously arriving into their hands? The stereotypical gamer is a social outsider with a strong sense of belonging to a subculture with its own values. Why should he risk appearing to collude with establishment figures by questioning the very thing which he and his friends hold most dear?

Finally, what if, when you actually get down to it – is it possible? – videogames should turn out to be less wonderful than you'd always thought?

Ever since we ate the apple in the Garden of Eden, according to the story of Genesis, we've been pulled in two directions: desiring both to know and to regain a state of innocence. Those pleasures which are most needful for us may also be the ones we fear to examine too closely. The celebrity stripped of reputation and glamour is a painful loss of illusion for fans. Alternatively, we accept we're in it for good and bad, warts and all. By studying what we love, we hope to deepen our appreciation and discover new levels of pleasure, even if these entail new pains. This way lies self-understanding, the traditional goal of philosophy.

Videogames pose exactly this choice because they symbolize childhood joy and escape from adult responsibilities. Dare we risk spoiling with too much thought the pleasures that games give us?

Know your pleasure principle

It's your birthday and you've been promised a night out. Where do you hope your friends will take you?

    A. The local bowling alley.

    B. A smart casino.

    C. The new rollercoaster ride at a nearby theme-park.

    D. A murder-mystery night at your favorite restaurant.

What's your idea of a perfect gaming moment?

    A. Executing a combination move that knocks out your opponent just when you're down to your last health point.

    B. Watching the roulette ball drop on your number.

    C. Trancing out to a psychedelic shooter on a giant screen with surround-sound speakers.

    D. After several months, completing the final quest of an epic role-playing game.

You're on a long journey and have packed a friend's handheld by mistake. This friend has terrible taste, and all the games are dismal. It's a hard choice. Which will you play?

    A. A sub-*Jurassic Park* dinosaur-versus-dinosaur fighting game.

    B. *Ultimate Card Games* compilation.

    C. A bizarre Japanese rhythm game.

    D. A pet simulator where you must look after puppies.

You answered mostly

A – You're *so* competitive! A head-to-head, winner-takes-all, sore loser. You like nothing better than proving who's best.

B – Your biggest thrill comes from striking it lucky. It's chance, not skill, that really excites you. You'd wager your grandmother's life savings.

C – You're really into speed and disorientation. Basically you get a kick out of anything that turns you upside-down and sends your head spinning.

D – You love to enter fictional and fantasy worlds. You spent most of yesterday questing in the company of a gnome and a mage, and you probably love to dress up.

Actually no gamer is purely any one of these cartoon profiles. Some people do have overriding preferences, but most of us enjoy different experiences on different occasions. Women's magazine-style questionnaires aren't meant to be taken too seriously. Psychological profilers, on the other hand, do use multiple-choice tests, comparable in format to the above, as primary instruments to help decide nontrivial questions, such as which candidate gets the job. They might argue that even our most flippantly expressed preferences reveal important truths about us, truths we may not recognize ourselves.

The four categories used in our example were identified by the French intellectual Roger Caillois in the 1950s. They've become standard among academics and designers for describing some basic differences between games. His terms come from Classical Greek and Latin: *agôn*, meaning contest or combat, *alea*, meaning dice, *ilinx*, the whirlpool, and *mimesis*, imitation or representation. Caillois explains each category using examples from sports and playground games, but they can also be applied to videogames.

In practice most games provide a combination of competition, chance, disorientation, and make-believe. Playing the first-person shooter *Call of Duty*, for example, you could at various moments focus intensely on outsmarting an opponent, recklessly go out all-guns-blazing, reel from the speed of a death-match, or identify with the characters in a cinematic sequence.

Various people have proposed alternative categories. The designer Richard Bartle, for example, suggests that role-playing gamers are mostly achievers, explorers, socializers, or killers. Playing along with millions of others in the sword 'n' sorcery *World of Warcraft*, you may take most pleasure from one-hundred-percent completion of a particular quest, or from wandering about discovering new places within the world, or from chatting and participating in a guild (club) meeting, or from slaying creatures and defeating other players. Probably you *can* enjoy all four kinds of activity, but one of them is the main thing that repeatedly draws you back and determines your overall experience and judgment of the game.

Recall occasions when the pleasure of competition, chance, disorientation, or make-believe was at its peak for you, when it filled your entire being and expressed your greatest joy in life. What were moments when you took it to excess, when it got you into trouble, when you lived up to the associated stereotype of the ruthless competitor, reckless gambler, adrenalin junkie, or fantasy freak? Or when these same impulses led to a breakthrough achievement for you, through a moment of heart-and-soul commitment and stepping-over of boundaries?

There may be no saying *why* one person is a compulsive risk-taker while their neighbor is a theatrical socialite. Depending on the culture in which you live, there may be no associated value judgment to these differences, either, especially if we're talking only about what you do for fun in your leisure time. Yet the kind of play you find most fulfilling is also a clue to what motivates you at a deep level. Caillois' four categories of play are also psychological types. Seemingly simplistic, they provide a means to understand the obscure, fundamental urge within you to make the most out of life – without which you'd ultimately have no reason to care, to strive, to play your part in the world, or perhaps even to get up in the morning.

Keep a gamer's diary

Another day's gaming over.

How will historians in the future know what it's like to be a gamer today? Long after you and I are dust, physical objects such as game consoles and disks will survive to tell some of our stories. The deeds of the great and famous, including perhaps some outstanding designers, will find their own way into the records through official documents and the sheer volume of material about them. Social history, by contrast, requires other kinds of evidence. What we know about the day-to-day life of a Roman soldier on Hadrian's wall, for example, derives from archaeological odds and ends, such as scraps of letters which happen to have survived.

Mostly what survives of ordinary people's ordinary lives is a matter of chance. Diaries are one way to improve the odds. Famous diaries, such as Anne Frank's and Samuel Pepys', witness extraordinary moments in history or simply record their times with such vividness that they become compelling for people in other ages. No period or aspect of human history is devoid of interest. It just needs to find its chronicler.

The diaries of teenage girls stereotypically report crushes, fallings-out, fashion and personal-beauty triumphs or disasters, parental injustices, and other lonely confidences. Doubtless these will be of some interest to future historians. First, they'll have recurrent themes, including information about the writers' perspective as a social class. Second, their incidental details, such as passing mentions of what's happened in the news, will reveal larger matters of whose historical importance the writer may at the time be largely unaware. Third, individual examples will possess unusual clarity and intelligence, reveal distinctive personality, or explore atypical themes.

The same would presumably apply to gamers' diaries, should a significant number be written or recorded. This may already be happening without being publically known. We should expect videogames to feature in many people's diaries as a regular leisure activity and source of achievements, frustrations, and aspirations. What we'd qualify as a *gamer's* diary would have more specific focus on these and related matters to the exclusion of others, together with a more self-conscious purpose in its recording and reflection.

On a larger scale, autobiographies and memoirs may likewise feature gaming in passing or as a major formative influence and theme. These documents are typically produced in later life and may develop out of diaries, with which they share some motivations, such as the desire to record and understand your own life. No gamer can yet undertake more than a few decades' retrospective of a life in videogames, but this will gradually change.

Great diaries are often marked by a compelling honesty, fearless of disapproval but not interested in gaining popularity either. This is a key difference between private diaries and blogs written in the hope of gaining an audience. When you sincerely expect your diary to reach no-one except yourself – or at least no-one who can in the smallest way benefit or harm you – you're freed to say absolutely whatever you want. This only becomes meaningful, however, if you take the opportunity to explore what's normally unsayable and therefore repressed or unnoticed. The question then is, what are the usual taboos and silences in gamers' talk, both between and to themselves?

What's not required is a series of daily essays. Diaries typically filter everything through the individual's direct, personal experience. Historians of the future will want to know how it feels like for you to live through the times. Honesty must extend to your own feelings and reactions, which can be notoriously hard to face. As well as the external facts of your day-to-day gaming life, what are some of the inner experiences? How do games enter your dreams and daydreams, for example?

Don't underestimate the historical value of seemingly trivial information. From a literary viewpoint, too, readers are interested as much in the everyday normality of other people's lives as in the high-points. Certainly it helps to be able to tell a story, and to make one out of the stuff of daily life – in other words, what we normally allow to pass by as mundane and unworthy of special notice. This is very different from the efficient logging of mission briefings that's called a journal in many videogames. You'll also aim at something more substantial than the 'status updating' of Twitter and Facebook.

The project of keeping a gamer's diary requires something of a turn away from the usual gaming attitude, in so far as that's oriented towards immersing yourself in play and flowing from one game to the next. Like the reviewer or blogger, the diarist pauses in order to turn reflective; he or she lays down the controller and prepares to type, or hand-write, or make a voice or video recording.

A diarist does this once every day or as near that as possible. This regular rhythm, as in religious devotions, after a while provides its own habitual support for the writer. The *day*, with its miniature lifecycle from awakening's birth to sleep's death, becomes your unit of meaning in thinking about your life's journey. Gamers' reputed habit of late-night playing may therefore help or hinder the keeping of a diary, whose entries are conventionally made at the end of each day, shortly before going to bed. Your mind is active till late, but if your days regularly blur into nights and thence into each other then how can you keep a daily diary? Perhaps you might keep a noctary instead (from *nox*, Latin for night, whereas diary comes from *die*, day).

You might experiment with keeping a diary for a short, trial period. This could be a useful aid to studying your experience of a particular game or to preparing for an academic or journalistic piece. To become a Diarist, though, you'll need to keep at it. The solar year, with its seasonal cycle of spring's birth to winter's death, is a natural next unit in scale up from the day. Over this timescale you'll become like the keeper of an animal with demands and a lifespan of its own.

Your diary might also become a keep like those inside medieval castles, such as the Tower of London, built to hold precious or dangerous items securely – hence the locks that adorn some journals you can buy. I suspect these mostly flatter the writer's sense of self-importance. Most of us don't have such great secrets, just a desire for privacy.

For the foreseeable future, you'll probably have little to gain among other gamers by keeping a diary. People won't know you're at it, or their curiosity might not stretch beyond asking whether they make a personal appearance. You won't have anything substantial to show until later, and possibly not even then. Instead you might settle for the subtle changes to your character and outlook that develop from becoming a confirmed diarist, and for the satisfaction of knowing there's a chance your words will one day be read as part of the record of a period in history.

Episode 2: The Innermost Cave

Unpick the hook and bathe in the after-glow

First impressions count. In a crowded cultural marketplace, every videogame, film, book, television channel, pop song, magazine advertisement, and shopping-mall store must vie for your attention. It may have only a moment's glance or a few minutes of your time to sink its hooks into your heart and reel you in. *Try me, I'm what you want. See, already I'm giving you what you need and we've only just started. There's lots more where this came from. I promise you're going to love this…*

You can guarantee that the opening sections of any professionally-produced videogame will have had great care lavished upon them. The designers know they must get it right. By examining the opening in detail (a process known as close reading or close playing) you can uncover some of their key design choices and reasoning. This may be easier with the help of a video recording, such as those available on YouTube, which you can pause and rewind. The closer your examination, the more your attention resembles that given by the designers during all their hours of labor in the studio. Assume that nothing is accidental and that every detail, no matter how small, has been chosen with a purpose.

What constitutes the opening varies widely from one game to another. For arcade games it's the rolling screens designed to tempt us to drop the coin in the slot and then the first section of gameplay. In today's console and computer games, the title sequence typically establishes a back-story or introduces the game's fictional world and characters, for example through a glossy cinematic followed by a tutorial. For an epic role-playing game that may take several weeks or longer to complete, does the opening consist of the first four minutes of play, the first four hours, or the first four days and nights? Watching trailers, studying box art, and reading reviews also prime you to play, so these might count as part of the opening, too.

Really all you're trying to establish is: what's the hook and how has it caught you? What lures you to step inside the magic circle and start playing the game? What's the pleasure you're seeking, and what fulfillment do you hope to gain? With a sequel or a game that comes with a high recommendation, you may be hooked well in advance. With an untried game, it's likely to be a combination of marketing, your initial experience of gameplay, and perhaps how much you paid for it that determines whether you're motivated to carry on past the opening levels.

Maybe the beginning will be a dramatic set-piece showcasing the best the item has to offer. This is like wearing your sexiest outfit on the first date or starting a firework display with a mega-rocket. Alternatively the beginning may present a single small but telling detail signaling much greater things to come: a song that starts quietly, an exquisite appetizer that's gone in two mouthfuls. Like the hare and tortoise, both strategies have their advantages and risks. Showy openings create immediate excitement which may then lead to ultimate disappointment. Underwhelming introductions may lose their audience before they get round to slow-building a powerful finale. The former takes the money up-front, so to speak, whereas the latter aims for customer loyalty.

A great opening is no guarantee of success. A concert, meal, sports match, or election campaign needs to do more than start well. As the saying goes, it's not how you start it's how you finish. Many videogames, including beat-'em-ups and shooters, provide clear win-lose conditions as well as incentives to go on improving your skills and pitting yourself against ever-tougher opponents. In coin-op arcade games you lose your last life and receive your final score, which is a number always capable of being higher next time around. In so-called persistent worlds, such as *World of Warcraft*, our online characters may in principle continue questing indefinitely. Other games have prominent storylines which reach an ending as definite as any film: we defeat the ultimate boss, and the closing credits roll. In this case you can analyze the last few sections of the game to see how the designers lead you into a final heightened emotional state. Increasingly, though, even games with a definite storyline are conceived from the outset to enable a sequel and, with luck, an endlessly profitable franchise. You'll be left wanting more.

What counts as the ending is therefore as ragged and varied as what counts as the opening. The ending of anything may leave us with a feeling of satisfaction, completion, resolution, and closure, or of frustration, unfinished business, unanswered questions, unfulfilled potentials, unhealed wounds, and rankling injustice. This especially applies to games that have engrossed us and made us really care.

Endings relate back to beginnings. They deliver on the promise made at the opening. In any storytelling medium, endings may also have the function of rewarding the good characters – in most videogames that's us, the player – and punishing the bad, our enemy or rival. Poetic justice (a.k.a. comeuppance and just desserts) tends to show what should ideally happen rather than what actually does happen in real life. The villain is usually not allowed to get away with his crimes and must often die a spectacularly gruesome death. Some endings feel 'right' and believable while others fail to convince. Endings may be happy or sad, simple or complex, optimistic or pessimistic. Videogames, with their escapist function and lack of social realism, rarely dare to attempt anything truly tragic or bleakly downbeat. Personally I have a taste for bittersweet endings, a combination of romance and realism where the hero wins what he originally wanted but loses something which turns out to be equally, if not more, precious. This is a recipe some game writers try to follow when planning their storylines for maximum emotional impact.

As a medium that in part aims to break away from traditional, linear models of storytelling inherited from older, 'non-interactive' media such as novels and films, videogames question the very principle of endings that has shaped creative production for centuries. Make-believe endings relate in some way to those we experience in real life. Sharing the triumphs and defeats of beloved characters, whether in games, television soap operas, or graphic novels, provides shape and meaning for our own lives. Ultimately this can lead us to contemplate both personal death and the apocalypse, or end of time itself. What, then, if there is no definite end?

In one way, ending is inevitable even if you prefer games that are in principle open-ended, since at some point we must always pause playing – in order to go to the bathroom, to bed, or to work. So, after pausing or finishing a game that you've particularly enjoyed playing, allow yourself to savor the after-glow: the rich brew of feelings, generated by the game, that stays with you and colors your mood. You're in love. Part of you bursts to share your thoughts with other people. Another part wants only to hug your feelings in private in the hope of maintaining their intensity away from the light of broad day, in which they must inevitably fade (a little death). Maybe you delay the ending as long as you can by stretching out the moment, or return to the start and play it through all over again. How far are you able to recapture the high or maintain the glow you felt the first time around? What's no longer the same?

Even if your feelings turn into a sadness for the gradual passing of what the game's ending has wrought within you, decide not to dive straight into the next game to escape this discomfort. Savor the melancholy. Hold the pain close as proof that you *can* feel, that you are alive, and that videogames at their finest are capable of stirring the soul.

Invite a character home

Bruised yet elated, the victors at last go off-duty, for the game is over. Doors close behind them, they shrug off their armor and start to relax. Sonic the Hedgehog, who cannot normally bear to stand still, lays aside the watch that he taps whenever the player is momentarily idle, adopts the lotus position, and starts to meditate. Ultra-butch Marcus Fenix dons an apron and starts to weigh sugar for brownies. Nathan Drake, fortune-hunter and free-climber extraordinaire, picks up Aristotle's *Nichomachean Ethics* and continues reading where he left off.

Alan Moore and Dave Gibbons' groundbreaking graphic novel, *Watchmen*, showed us in a realistic manner what superheroes might get up to when not battling villains in cape and tights. They, too, it turns out, must fix supper and attend to the laundry. Videogame characters, for the most part, likewise appear to us so rarely in their ordinary lives that to imagine these is necessarily a jolt. Of course there are exceptions: the Sims, Billy in the school game *Bully* (a.k.a. *Canis Canem Edit*), your cute cartoon-animal homemaker in *Animal Crossing*. These are hardly realistic, however. In each case, 'ordinary life' has been redesigned so as to be fun-to-play. The same applies to role-playing games, such as *Fable*, which allow the player to take time off from the main campaign to buy and furnish a home, to develop a romantic life and social skills. We can still wonder what the player-characters would do if they could ever leave the stage-set of the game-world and escape players' surveillance by closing the door to some inner, private room.

As a primarily visual medium, videogames must use a variety of techniques to suggest their characters' inner world of thoughts and feelings (interiority). These techniques, many of them borrowed from film, include music, lighting, symbols, body-language, and more explicit statements such as voiceovers, diary entries, and dream or vision sequences. A recent innovation occurs in the murder-mystery game, *Heavy Rain*. The loading screen between levels presents a tight close-up on the face of the character we're about to play, lit in unflattering detail against a black background. As we wait for play to resume, we examine his or her features, watch the character look around as if in a private moment of uncertainty, and imagine the consciousness going on behind the mask.

When characters constitute a form of intellectual property and function as brand mascots, their owners defend them staunchly. Slash fictions, which imagine same-sex relationships between iconic characters, such as *Star Trek*'s Captain Kirk and First Officer Spock, may thus face legal action by the copyright holders.

In cosplay, fans begin to inhabit their favorite character's persona by dressing up and posing. Their aim is to recreate the character as he or she exists within the fictional game-world, but necessarily there's a clash (some might say comical) between the intended illusion and the all-too visible reality of ill-fitting spandex and starkly-lit conference centers.

The desire to debunk heroes has quite a long heritage. In the nineteenth century, realism was a widespread movement to modernize the arts. Painters and novelists especially sought to attack idealized and romanticized visions of what the world is like and to show what really happens. In truth we are not heroes, says the realist, determined to spare us no delusion. We cannot stay young forever. Marriage is rarely the happily-ever-after we've been told. War is horrific and futile, not glorious. The vast majority of us will never be fabulously rich. Good doesn't always triumph, and there's no sign yet of the meek inheriting the Earth. In each case, the realist would have us face up to a hard lesson: recognize the material conditions we actually inhabit, and their political foundations, and then get angry enough to do something about them. The purpose of heroes is in fact not to save the world but to keep us distracted from the difficult task of changing it for the better by ourselves.

This is an unpopular message. As many action-adventure games and Hollywood action movies prove, there's a thriving market for super-good-looking heroes who always win no-matter what the odds. It seems that most of us want to believe in these heroes, however unrealistic they may be as role-models.

Episode 2: The Innermost Cave

When you imagine a favorite game character visiting your home, your first thought may be to set them in another fantasy that pleases you, for example one where they take you with them back into the fictional world of the game. To imagine a game character becoming genuinely ordinary is difficult. Partly this is because we'd prefer them to remain as characters of fantasy, whom we can follow into a more exciting world than our own. More importantly, game characters are out of place in the real world. In some cases, the fictional world they inhabit lies on another planet, in the future, or in an alternate universe, so that in our everyday world they're alien visitors. Or if they were once human and from our world, they've lost all of their ordinariness and been changed utterly by their adventures. If they attempt to retire, life will inevitably disappoint, wounds will fester, or one last campaign will beckon. Look at the difficulties facing war-veterans on return to civilian life, or those who've lost their former fame and become, as the stereotype goes, bitter, drunken, washed-up has-beens. Once a hero, always a hero.

As shown by the opening episode of the *Red versus Blue* machinima series, a satire on the massively popular first-person shooter *Halo*, when game characters stop to think what they're doing they're likely to have an existential crisis.

Two heavily armored soldiers stand idle in the middle of a hushed canyon. Birdsong. One turns to the other:

First soldier: Hey.

Second soldier: Yeah.

First soldier: You ever wondered why we're here?

Second soldier: It's one of life's great mysteries, isn't it: why are we here? I mean, are we the product of some cosmic coincidence, or is there really a God watching everything – you know, with a plan for us and stuff? I don't know, man, but it keeps me up at night.

First soldier: What?! I mean, why are we *out here in this canyon*.

Second soldier: Oh… I… Yeah.

First soldier: Well, what's all that stuff about God?

Second soldier: Ah…

First soldier: Hm?
Second soldier: Nothing.
First soldier: You want to talk about it?

We unheroic mortals must find contentment in our mundane lives. By inviting a videogame hero into our own home, we may offer them a special kind of hospitality. Consider the celebrity who searches for a place where he won't be recognized, or the billionaire seeking to be loved for herself and not for her fortune. Each tries to find something elusive in their world yet which is freely available to everyone else and thus taken for granted. Welcoming someone into your home, a place unique in all the world, can be one of the most precious gifts to offer. Badger your illustrious guest to tell of their great adventures in the world of games – or see afresh those modest, overlooked things in your domestic life that would touch your guest with gratitude, envy, and joy.

What will you offer them to eat and for entertainment? Where will you show them on the tour of your home and neighborhood? What will you learn about your guest's private self, for better and for worse during their stay? What will you learn about yourself from the way they respond to your home?

Become cyborg

Think humans will always be the greatest sporting champions? The RoboCup project aims by 2050 to develop a team of 'fully autonomous humanoid robot soccer players' capable of defeating the human team which has won the most recent World Cup. Maybe, then, a robot will one day walk in, sit down right next to you, take up the controller, and beat you at your favorite videogame. Computers already play chess better than most humans, after all, and it's standard for videogames to be populated by computer-controlled opponents whose abilities can be increased to test even the most proficient player.

A videogaming robot would presumably need to combine artificial intelligence software with electronics and moving parts in order to gather sensory input (primarily light and sound) from the game; analyze this input; calculate responsive actions; and perform these actions via the game's controls – all in real time. To become a champion, it would need to perform some, if not all of these tasks better than humans.

In the *robot versus human* playoff, where do you think the robot might win? To put this another way, when you play a videogame how are *you* robot-like, and how could a machine improve on your performance? For example, in a platform game it might take you a dozen or more attempts before you can coordinate an especially tricky sequence of jumps, dodges, crouches, and jumps. By the time you succeed, you might begin to feel something like a machine. Robots and computers famously outperform humans at repetitive work.

And where, if anywhere, might you expect the human to defeat the robot? Or in other words, when you play, in which parts of the game do you feel most human and least machine-like?

However you answer these last two questions, know that AI and robotics experts look upon the simulation of *any* given aspect of human mental and physical performance as so many scientific and technical problems waiting to be solved. Chauffeur, housemaid, tennis partner, child's playmate – we can design a robot (or android) for that, eventually. And then a surgeon, a pianist, a politician, a lover…

Arguably scientists' most difficult challenge is to model how humans make meaning out of their experience, since this is notoriously complex and based on many factors, including personal history, embodiment, and social and cultural influences – how you were educated, what you ate for breakfast today, and who your friends are. Hence scientists still have a long way to go in developing systems capable of true natural language processing – that is, enabling computers to understand and participate in everyday speech of moderate complexity, not just to process a preset list of verbal commands (as some in-car satellite-navigation systems do, with varying degrees of success). Precisely because of this computational complexity, videogames tend not to make natural language central to their gameplay. Dialogue in games is usually all preprogrammed in one way or another, so that in most cases robots could in fact make sense of it without needing the wider understanding and personality provided by actual life experience.

I'm therefore left wondering how many videogames really require a human being, not just a robot, to play them.

Of course this isn't the same as enjoying them. So far as we know, no computer has ever enjoyed playing chess – whereas many humans enjoy playing at being computer- or robot-like.

In the figure of the *cyborg*, human and machine blend into a new organism. Like robots, cyborgs are creatures familiar firstly from science fiction and secondly from news stories about the latest scientific and technological research. In other words cyborgs are both a fantasy and a reality.

In the real world they are you and I: people whose relationships with everyday technologies, whether pacemaker implants, prosthetic limbs, contact lenses, mobile telephones, or game consoles, have become increasingly intimate and interdependent.

In our fantasies this hybrid creature often has an element of the superhuman, possessing enhanced powers and pioneering a future where we have become one with our technologies. Equally, cyborgs may appear monstrous, having lost their humanity, and are therefore to be feared. In our fictions and nightmares, the closeness between ourselves and our technologies grows extreme, such that flesh flows seamlessly into metal and digital data streams directly into nerves. Those never-removed headphones might as well plug directly into the brain; as machines invade the body so do they invade the mind and personality.

Gamers have firsthand experience of what it feels like to be a cyborg. Human anatomy comprises head, torso, limbs, sense organs, and so on, yet when we immerse ourselves in playing a videogame our thumbs seem to become attached to the controller, our eyes to the screen, and our bladders belong to someone we've temporarily ceased to be. Muscle merges with electronics and our conscious awareness is filled with the fictional game-world. Some new, composite being is born. Its cyborg body, partly human and partly machine, thrills with a ceaseless flow of sensation, information, and desire. We're taken out of ourselves and become something less mundane and more adventurous. We know exactly what to do because we've internalized the game's logic and become its ideal processor of information about incoming obstacles, resource depletion, routes to target, tactical deployment, weapon selection…

Do you recognize yourself as something of a cyborg? (Note that one reason for hesitating to identify with the cyborg might be a fear this would reinforce existing negative stereotypes about gamers.)

While playing a game, notice if and when the 'cyborg effect' occurs. Which parts of your anatomy seem to merge with the game system, or which parts of your onscreen character or environment seem to become extensions of your own body? What are the pleasures of this experience?

Who are the cyborg characters portrayed in videogames, and how are these fun for you to play or to fight? How much of your cyborg self lies in the realm of wish-fulfillment and make-believe, and how much in the reality of your physical integration with the game system?

Practice the inner game

Sport coaches must work on players' mental as well as physical performance. In games such as tennis and golf, players may strike the ball perfectly one hundred times in a row during practice yet go to pieces under the pressure of a match. Their nerves get the better of them. What such players need in order to attain peak performance is to practice how to think well, for example using techniques pioneered by Tim Gallwey.

Learn to silence the mental chatter, often self-critical, which distracts your body from performing in the ways it knows best.

Switch off your concentration when it's not needed – break the tension with a laugh – and intensely back on for moment-by-moment awareness of your body, your racquet or club, and the ball.

Train yourself to respond positively to certain behavioral triggers, such as pinching together your thumb and forefinger, which you've preassociated with positive emotions.

Gamers might benefit from this approach in so far as gaming can be a performance sport. This applies most obviously to competitive multiplayer genres, such as fighting, racing, and shooters, which test players' perceptual and motor skills in match-like conditions.

Inner gaming doesn't stop there, however. Some gamers view every session, whatever the genre, as an occasion to prove and improve their performance. If you're the kind of person who always wants to win, then you'll already recognize the description given above of how you need to master your excitement during competition. Assuming every move potentially contributes to victory, you notice every detail of play and stay highly focused on achieving your goal.

Even if you're not competitive in this way and prefer less performance-intensive types of play, most videogames contain at least moments of challenge designed to test your abilities. Else why play at all? When you keep falling into the same pit, must choose between continued attack or strategic retreat, hurry to collect all the pieces against the clock, or try to outrun the police – in these moments your ability to perform comes into the spotlight. You know what's at stake and how it could all go wrong. You must hold your nerve. Videogames are designed, through tutorials and structured levels, to prepare you so you can succeed at such challenges, often without having to think too much about it. On a micro scale, without your realizing it, they train you to play the mental as well as the physical game.

It's possible to play many videogames internally in another way, too. For many years I practiced Tai Chi and gradually understood what my teachers told me, that the graceful, slow-motion, martial-arts movements occur simultaneously inside and outside, in the mind and in the body. All at once, you *imagine* (or is that *remember*?) your arm moving, *feel* it moving as you would if your eyes were closed, *move* it, and *see* it moving with your peripheral vision. It's then possible to practice the movement by performing only the first of these actions (imagining, remembering) while you sit perfectly still at your desk.

Start with a particular sequence of movements that you've been performing in a videogame, such as steering through a tricky corner, run-turn-jumping to reach a high ledge, or executing a special combination move. Choose something that you wish to perform better. Having attempted it many times, you'll be able to visualize the movement occurring onscreen and recall the controls required to produce the movement. So now imagine (remember) performing the movement – with your eyes open or closed, with your hands moving or still, touching the controls or not – but *without* actually pressing the controls. In other words, mentally rehearse. Combine this exercise with actually playing the sequence and notice if it makes any obvious or subtle differences to your performance.

Don't expect instant results, though perhaps these might occur. As in many Eastern martial-arts and meditational systems, your aim is gradually to attain a relaxed yet highly attentive poise, where your mind is calm and your body flows effortlessly through familiar or improvised movements. Videogames necessarily require action – if the player does nothing with the controls play soon comes to a halt – yet action needn't imply agitation, adrenalin-rush, or mindlessness. Indeed, what's most visible about champion gamers in action is precisely their mental focus and physical calm.

Initially it might seem that the easiest videogames to relax to are those which resemble digital toys, where you wander among beautifully-rendered open worlds, tend to an artificial garden or pet, or arrange objects into geometric patterns. By placing low demands on the player such games verge on boredom, which can indeed be a welcome relief after a hectic day's work. Alternatively you might prefer the trance offered by musical shooters such as *Rez* and *Geometry Wars*, where you're kept busy but are able to leave the mundane world behind in a repetitive, pulsing, psychedelic lightshow.

Most difficult to play in a Zen-like manner are those games deliberately designed to unnerve and agitate: survival horror and shooter death-matches, say. These games systematically terrorize through fear and shock tactics and pitch you into a whirlwind of kill-or-be-killed activity. To move gracefully through their worlds, to maintain mental poise at your still center and meet every obstacle with a swift yet unhurried response, requires a different order of relaxed attention from playing digital toys or trance games. When all those around you run deranged, you keep your cool.

Many videogames have begun to simulate this experience through the cinematic convention, first popularized by the *Matrix* films, known as bullet-time. At the press of a button, the world pauses while your character makes a leisurely inspection of the bullet fired from the enemy's gun and now hanging in midair. This is a visual metaphor for the martial artist's poise under pressure.

Your choice, then: whether to experience this poise secondhand as a readily-available image onscreen, or whether to begin the training that might bring you moments of this poise firsthand as a direct, unmediated experience.

Observe your body playing

Judging from YouTube, quite a few gamers enjoy creating a video record of their playing performances. Usually the camera points at the screen and not at the player. Gameplay is captured via a digital camcorder, a DVD recorder wired between console and television monitor, or using screen-capture software on a personal computer. What the player's body may be doing is left out of these loops except as the actions it performs within the game via the controls.

When gamers do appear in person in front of the camera, this is more often to give an amusing presentation to a game review, as if they're auditioning for the role of television presenter. We still don't get to see what they look like at the moment when they're playing.

What's to see? you might ask. Someone twitching at a few controls, staring in concentration, and grimacing when things go wrong. Such off-screen drama surely pales before the spectacle onscreen, and even that, notoriously, is far less interesting to watch than it is to play yourself.

Yet in other circumstances watching a video of people you know and especially of yourself retains a power to fascinate and often to appall. Do I really look and sound like *that*? Even decades after home-movie-making first became widely affordable, even now that webcams and video-capable mobile phones are commonplace, videos of yourself can still shock with their apparent truth-telling. We don't all rehearse regularly in front of the camera in preparation for fame. The video image of ourselves remains a partial stranger, especially when a side or rear view rather than the frontal view we see in the mirror and in talking-straight-to-camera facial shots.

Sit with friends or family to watch a home video and there's often a potential for embarrassment. Prepare to cringe and be laughed at. When a person's behavior is caught on camera, even those who know them well may be taken aback: they never realized you walked quite like that. The camera's eye sees all sorts of details usually missed, which become potential telltale signs of secret thoughts. At the time the video was made, none of you realized you were under such surveillance.

For this reason, video footage is a staple source of information for psychologists about what goes on inside people's heads, about their personal relationships and body-language. Video a couple who've just argued, and a psychologist will find numerous clues in the recording to the emotional conflict simmering between them. Many of these clues will operate at a subconscious level. In the resentful silence, one scowls with arms crossed while the other bites the corner of a lip.

When you watch a video of your body playing a videogame, it may take some time to tune in to the small scale of the information available. In the early part of the recording your behavior may be skewed by self-consciousness of the camera – you glance towards or deliberately ignore it. Typically this effect diminishes later in the recording. Now and then an obvious gesture occurs: you sigh, or look away from the game, or wince, or lean forward, or your eyes become suddenly busy, or a cry bursts forth. But even when nothing significant appears to be happening, it's possible to notice and interpret ever finer movements implying minute shifts in your attitude towards the game: a blink, a flinch.

Ideally you'll have a recording of the gameplay to watch as well, synchronized with the video of your body. This takes some doing, which is probably why so few examples appear online. Even without this, it's usually possible to identify some key moments in the game from the soundtrack, your visible reactions, and memory of what happened when you played.

As I said, if you're unused to seeing yourself on camera in this way it doesn't take much to produce at least a small shock. The recording will be eye-opening as if you're spying on yourself.

With greater methodological sophistication, psychologists often use this kind of observation, focusing on the player rather than the game, to study videogame 'effects.' As much as what happens onscreen, what matters is what the game appears to do to the gamer and how he or she reacts to it.

There's no need to watch only yourself, of course. The next time you have the opportunity (or misfortune?) to watch someone else play, try paying less attention to what's happening onscreen. There's so much to see and wonder over in the person of the gamer, if you can tune in to this. As psychologists, sociologists, actors, and novelists can tell you, human behavior is endlessly fascinating and revealing.

Greet your boredom

Nothing's happening. Time has slowed to a crawl and life is passing you by while you just sit waiting. You could be out there having experiences that count as really living – things you'd be proud to have done. Not this hanging around aimlessly, feeling empty and vaguely dissatisfied. You're not hungry or in pain, so have no real reason to complain. It's just that you're wasting what should be precious time. All too soon it'll be over and you'll have achieved nothing except feel miserable. Ah, give me something new, something to carry me away!

One of the main purposes of play is simply to pass the time. If we've nothing better to do, a game will entertain us. We're invited as guests and can stay for as long as it takes for the bus to arrive, or a friend we've arranged to meet, or sleep... The game rescues us from boredom, from facing blank time on our own. It keeps us company and enables us to amuse ourselves. Now we're doing something. We've exercised choice and taken action. We may not be having the greatest-ever experiences of our lives, but a bit of fun is a good-enough substitute for now and better than doing absolutely nothing.

Viewed negatively, this motivation for playing games is given the names of time-wasting and distraction. Supposedly we should be doing something more useful or beneficial with our time and selves: working out, earning, studying, praying, visiting elderly relatives, cleaning the house – any number of allegedly more worthwhile activities which, for now at least, we have no desire whatsoever to perform. Play is precisely a holiday from self-improvement and social contribution... which returns us to a life as enslaved as before we went on vacation. Play distracts us from facing the grim realities of our lives: our economic thralldom, political oppression, frustrated aspirations, fraught or frigid relationships, mortality, and so on. Arguably these are the actual causes of our dissatisfaction and what we should really be spending our precious free time trying to do something to change – if only we had the energy and wherewithal.

Here lies also a common distinction among gamers, between casual and hardcore. Microsoft's *Solitaire* and *Minesweeper* help occupy millions of deskbound lunch-breaks. This year's latest big-budget console games, by contrast, aim to provide spectacular intensity of experience. There's nothing boring about them.

Boredom has both a personal and a social history. Probably people have always been bored, if in slightly different ways or for different reasons from today. Conventionally the special suffering of teenagers, housewives, the unemployed, office and factory workers, boredom is often a consequence of routinized divisions between work and leisure that require artificial switches in how we're expected to feel and behave, with no end in sight to the pattern of our weeks. Boredom is also the unappreciated luxury of those fortunate to live in relative material comfort, safe from hardships worse than boredom, removed from the urgent needs of others, and longing for a bit of adventure.

The last hundred-or-so years have seen industrial-scale production of entertainment for the masses, first in books and magazines, then radio, cinema, recorded music, television, and more recently videogames and the Internet. In each case, entertainment is offered as an external remedy, so to speak, against boredom. Preventative medicine, by contrast, lies in exploring your own creative expression and personal interests – whether in song, sport, or countless other activities. This way you'll never be bored, or so life-coaches tell us.

Many entertainment remedies are subject to the law of diminishing returns. This states that, above a certain level, increasing input yields declining benefits. A clichéd example is the junkie who needs ever larger or more frequent hits in order to attain a high. Hence gamers are stereotyped as compulsive addicts dependent on their next fix.

By contrast, skilled practice – learning a musical instrument, for an obvious example – continues to reward effort (and retains its boredom-preventing benefits) over a lifetime by enabling the practitioner to attain ever greater proficiency. The related image of gamers, as lifelong apprentices to a master craft, is less easy to find in the media.

Which of these two profiles – addict or apprentice – better matches your personal experience of gaming's relationship to boredom?

How is it that playing a boring game can be relaxing, refreshing, and healing in some way? Why do we become bored playing games which, on paper and according to the trailers, should thrill and delight us? We start to think of something else, are tempted to throw the game aside. Is it possible to be bored without noticing it?

Like any other aspect of existence, boredom is something you can choose to become more aware of, even *interested* in. It's a special opportunity to find out something about yourself. Perhaps imagine it's like holding your breath. As the boredom grows, as you continue to endure it, what's in danger of happening? Try to identify the *qualities* of your boredom: the physical and mental restlessness, the desire to be elsewhere and experience something new, the unwelcome exposure of your own inner emptiness or conflicts. Then when you start to play a game, notice the various sensations of relief, if these occur, or of failure and dissatisfaction continuing to possess you.

Measure your playing habits

You are a number. Or rather, you're many numbers to different institutions. To insurers, you're a set of risks expressed as mathematical probabilities. To your employer, you're a payroll number and a line in a salaries spreadsheet. To government departments, you're a driving license number, passport number, and health service number, among others. To legions of pollsters, data analysts, market researchers, and statisticians – including those working for the game industry – you're a fraction of a percentile.

Many online videogames collect statistical data about players. For games hosting millions of players worldwide at any one time (MMOGs), numerical analysis is essential for both day-to-day quality assurance and ongoing development. It's also now standard for videogames to present players with numerical information about their performance – such as the highest number of stealthy kills achieved in a row – indicating preferences in gameplay style and areas for potential improvement. You may choose to share such information online with other gamers as part of social networking. By recording your playing habits and achievements and comparing these against the wider world of gaming, you can find new games to suit your tastes and new sparring partners of a level to match your own.

One might easily become obsessed with measuring every facet of daily life. Electronic counters are readily available for the number of steps you take, calories you consume, and texts you send within any given twenty-four hour period. This might be a dehumanizing process distracting you from getting on with simply living by constant anxieties about too much of this or too little of that.

In themselves numbers are nothing to be scared of, though the Arts-Sciences cultural divide does unfortunately produce many people with deep dislike and ignorance of numbers. Politically they may be correct to suspect the uses to which statistics are put by organizations and the State. Bureaucrats too often reduce the complexity and suffering of real human beings to pie charts. Accustomed to scare-stories about themselves in the media, gamers are perhaps especially aware of how simplistic percentages can be abused. All this adds up to an argument in favor of becoming more numerate, so that you can interrogate and challenge the misapplication of statistical data.

Numbers can also be a route to self-understanding. One of the great insights of the social sciences is that human behavior *can* be understood numerically. Usually this understanding comes in terms of the mass. As individuals, we like to think we make decisions and choices freely. Social sciences explain, on the contrary, how much of our behavior is typical of our sex, age, race, economic class, religion, occupation, location, and so on. Commercially this insight leads to consumer profiling, targeted marketing, trend analysis and prediction. As individuals, meanwhile, we often can't access – or find difficult to accept – much of the statisticians' information about how we personally fit into various groups and what this might say about us.

You can to some extent take matters into your own hands by starting to track your own personal data, including your gaming habits. You might start by looking again at the data which videogames give you, such as the number of hours played, collectibles found, and heads shot. What do these say about you, rather than the game? Collate information across several games and ask the same question.

Then explore what other kinds of personal game-related data you might choose to collect for yourself. In most cases you'll have some idea of the area of behavior you wish to understand, so the task is then try to devise a relevant experiment. To take an obvious example, how are your hours of play distributed over the course of days, weeks, months, and seasons? How are they interspersed with other necessary activities, such as eating and sleeping? You already have a subjective sense of the answer to these questions. By collecting relevant numeric data, you'll obtain a potentially more objective perspective. Imagine, if you like, that the data refers to a different person. You're a scientist observing a specimen of the gaming population today.

There are many other aspects of your gaming life that you might investigate. Not everything can be found out through numerical recording and analysis, but quite a lot can, including things you might not have considered. As with any experiment, there's a chance that you'll make unexpected discoveries, or find nothing of interest.

Various helpful tools (app's) now exist online. If you also work with other gamers you'll be able to compare findings.

To extend this activity, investigate how to represent your personal data visually. I've seen a hundred ugly stupid graphs, but also many beautiful intelligent ones. Graphic designers have produced some superb examples of charts, maps, and diagrams that explain, tell stories, and reveal truths with startling clarity. It may be that you literally won't see what the figures you've gathered about yourself say until you try to show them visually.

And remember that explanation, storytelling, and discovery of truth are the aims of this mission. The numbers you collect will possess no value until you understand something about yourself through them.

Salivate, savor, digest

Food provides some of our most complete and reliable pleasures. Like sex, eating gives us a strikingly clear model of pleasure that we can apply to many other areas of life, including gaming.

Dining satisfies basic bodily needs of hunger, strengthens social union, and invites artistic appreciation. Each of us is an expert in the kinds of flavor, dish, and meal we enjoy. We look forward eagerly to the coming feast, whether midmorning treat, celebration dinner, or late-night takeout. Before we can sink our teeth into the food itself, delicious aromas arouse us with promises of intensity and perfection. We drool – the body preparing for the digestive work ahead. When we're at last able to consume the sweet or savory beauty, orgasmic releases flood through our bodies. We gorge, or appreciate every mouthful, or notice areas for improvement, or save the best piece till last. Maybe afterwards we'll feel sick, or hungry for more, or disappointed, or guilty. Ideally we'll feel deeply satisfied and ready to let the slow digestive process take over. We are content. Until, sooner or later, the process starts all over again. We start feeling hungry. When's the next meal? What shall it be this time? There's something new we've never tried before, or a taste from childhood that continues to elude us, or a trusty favorite we just fancy.

I could go on.

a. Note how your enjoyment of videogames occupies the past, present, and future. Most pleasures in fact consist of movements back and forth between the immediate present, memories of the recent and more remote past, and anticipation of what's soon or one day to come. Thus sexual pleasures include seduction, foreplay, and post-coital relaxation, as well as the act itself.

Consider your excitement during the buildup to a major videogame launch, the suspense as you hurry home from the store with a new game, how you look forward each day to that evening's session of play, or how you plan tactics for a particular level or match. The sense of release you feel when you actually get to play is all the more intense for the prior craving.

And what does that period of craving and suspense consist of but memories of your previous peak experiences of play, the prior history of the game series that lives within you, images recalled from trailers and advertisements that you've seen, and retrospective analysis of what you did right or wrong last time? From moment to moment as you play, your desire and ability to move forward and succeed rests on your knowledge of what you're aiming for and how to achieve it, knowledge that's supported by short- and sometimes longer-term memory. Despite the fast reactions that videogames often require, you need more than the limited memory-span of a goldfish to play any but the simplest games.

Likewise your whole sense of personal identity as a gamer – pleasure in who you are – rests on the particular combination of experiences you've built up during your years of play, resulting in certain tastes, areas of expertise and understanding shared with others, as well as your hopes for the future. This is true even if you're not a retro-gamer with a strong sense of nostalgia.

Do you take active delight in anticipation and suspense? How do you enjoy remembering without this becoming overly nostalgic?

b. The lifecycle of a pleasure takes place in both the mind and the body. On the one hand, puzzles and tactical or strategic problem-solving provide the most purely intellectual pleasures of gaming. Players across almost all genres enjoy the conscious glow of success and determination to try again or do better. On the other, videogames provide vivid sensory stimulation consisting primarily of sights, sounds, and movements made with the controls.

Any cycle of consumption entails a flow through the body. Though I didn't mention it earlier, elimination is an essential part of the eating cycle and ideally a bodily pleasure in its own right. Constipation, diarrhea, flatulence, indigestion, and vomiting – if you'll forgive mention of such unpleasantness – arise from disordered or poisoned flow. Gluttony, obesity, fasting, and starvation define the extremes of consumption, in terms not only of excess or lack but also economic power and personal choice.

The bodily symptoms of gorging on games (is there any danger of starvation?) will be variations on what happens when you consume either too much or too fast. Advertisers may want to force-feed gamers an unending feast of new titles, hurrying them to finish what they've only just bought so that the next can immediately be put before them, but surely you can't possibly keep up indefinitely. Are you worried there won't be enough to go round and you'll be left hungry? Can you pace yourself, or do you bolt and peak early? Are you a binger, and can you fast?

c. Pleasures are complicated by issues of social class and status, snobbery and assumptions about good taste. We don't hear much about videogame connoisseurs, whose super-refined palates can enjoy only the most rarified art-house and Japanese import games. Yet there are certainly gamers who turn their nose up at bestselling but mediocre sequels, or who specialize in a particular series or genre and have little time for newbies. Have you refined your palate as a gamer, in what ways are you a snob about games, and are you still able to enjoy simple tastes in gaming?

I'm not sure whether the videogames-as-food metaphor can ever be taken too far. What, for example, are the caffeine, low-carb mayonnaise, and caviar of games, the factory-farm, grandma's recipe, and television chef?

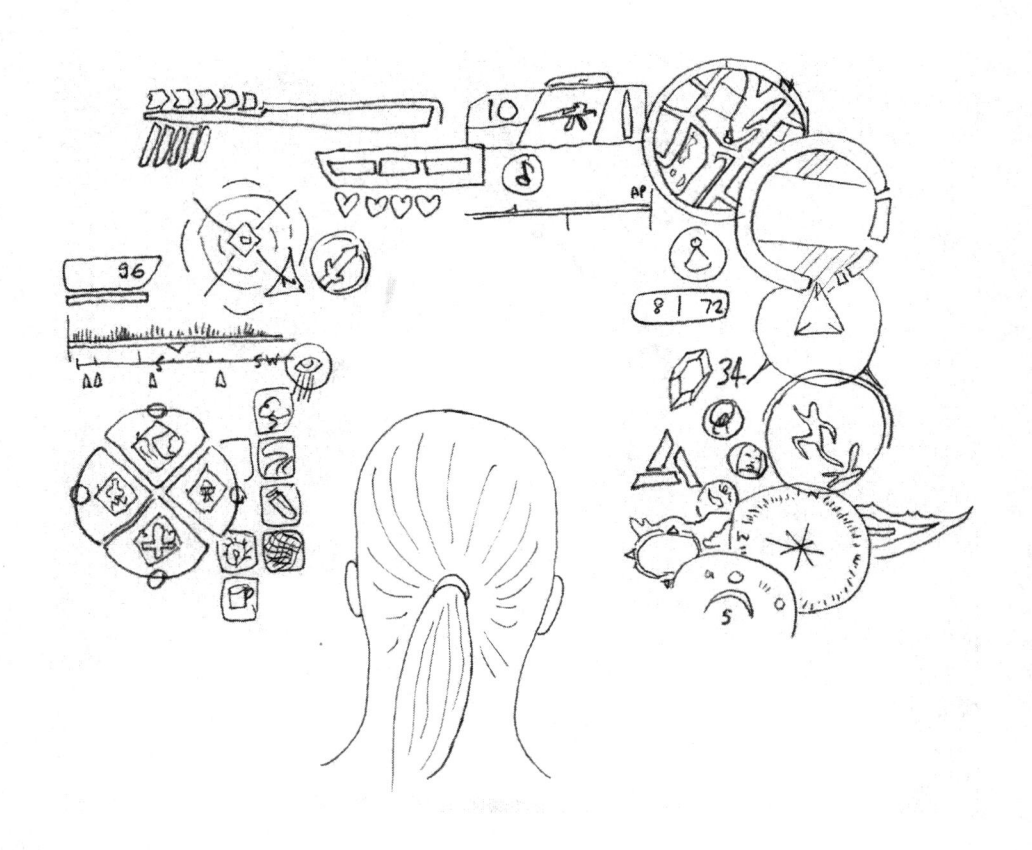

SIDE-QUESTS AND MINI-GAMES

Scholarly gaming

'Scholarly gamer' is not a contradiction in terms. The more common label of 'geek,' used both disparagingly and as a self-claimed identity, reflects a standoff between videogames and education that has only recently begun to ease through increasing recognition of the potential uses of games for learning. So many players possess such detailed knowledge, both of the games market as a whole and of preferred game series in particular, that one might wonder whether gamers are in fact – perhaps without fully realizing or wanting to acknowledge this – an unusually scholarly bunch.

Like the first writers of encyclopedias, players who write game-FAQs and walkthroughs must devote large periods of time to acquiring specialist knowledge through systematic study, accurate recording of information, exhaustive investigation, and 'book work' with electronic documents. The Internet provides abundant evidence of gamers applying the kind of uncompromisingly meticulous attention to detail that is elsewhere directed to the lifecycle of a rare species of butterfly or to the use of metaphor in some obscure medieval text. Applied to more traditional academic subjects, gamers' dedication would cheer many a schoolteacher who currently despairs of the alleged distractions by videogames from pupils' homework.

Of course it's possible that those players who go to the trouble of writing game-FAQs and walkthroughs are exceptional, both among gamers and their classmates. However, there seems to be quite widespread appreciation among gamers in general of the values of thoroughness and specialism. Both the Xbox 360 achievement and PlayStation 3 trophy systems have formalized the desire to complete games absolutely. This is more than just a desire to get your money's worth, I think. In the games you most love, there's nothing you don't want to know, no corner you won't explore, no side-quest or mini-game unworthy of your time. Such obsessive appetite for comprehensive knowledge of any given field is the hallmark of teenage fandom but also of academic scholarship.

Historically defined in relation to book-based learning within schools, scholarship has acquired a somewhat broader meaning. Colloquially (and sometimes sarcastically) it's possible to describe as a 'scholar' anyone who is highly learned in a subject, regardless of whether the subject or the means by which the learning was acquired is traditionally academic: a particularly knowledgeable, intellectually-inclined, and spectacles-wearing individual within a group of graffiti artists, say. Though fame awaits a few, all scholars must first and foremost be motivated as servants to their particular subject areas, or disciplines, which they strive, with some degree of selflessness, to organize, preserve, develop, advance, and disseminate against the forces of society and time that would otherwise sweep much of value into oblivion. Both within and across different subject areas, scholars act not just alone but in communities that share enduring values of intellectual rigor and social responsibility, which must be actively upheld. One of the scholar's main ongoing tasks is to find ways to explain and if need be justify their work in ways that non-specialists can understand.

The game-geek who wishes to become a game-scholar will embrace these principles. Currently there's a limit to how far this is possible, since institutional support is lacking from schools and other scholarly organizations, such as universities, museums, and institutes. You're therefore to some extent on your own when you tackle the following missions. These comprise 'odd jobs,' maybe not glorious in themselves but of service to the consolidation of Game Studies as an emerging subject.

Purify the language of the gamer tribe

So many videogames display the accolade 'masterpiece' on their front cover that one would think genius is in plentiful supply. We see the same claim made for books, films, albums, television dramas, and other mainstream entertainment. After a while you realize that in most cases nothing truly exceptional has occurred. Scores awarded by game reviewers have become similarly devalued currency, as many players complain. Overuse of nine-out-of-tens and other superlatives implies that game developers are already masters of their art – in other words, have almost nothing left to learn and approach perfection. Such self-congratulation betrays a lack of consensus as to how videogames might be substantially better.

Expressions such as 'awesome,' 'cool,' and 'fun' form an even more common language of admiration among players, as if their mere utterance justifies videogames' existence. Yet we might as well howl, purr, and whoop. As a critical vocabulary for discussing games, these terms amount to a slouching, even philistine disavowal of the need for precision. Ban them from your lips.

Frowning sternly, demand to know what specific meanings, if any, lie behind such clichés as 'mind-blowing,' 'eye-candy,' and 'visual feast.' The task of purifying the language of the tribe – originally a phrase to describe the function of poets – belongs not just to academics, reviewers, and those who write about videogames for a living. Gamers at large, who together already write millions of words online each year – several hundred too many, some might say – have a stake in sharpening their primary tools for articulating exactly what's so great about videogames. There may be some 'entertainment value' in reading 7/10 reviews and Top-Ten lists that are so lazily written you want to [insert chosen form of self-harm]. Yes, there is something comical about bad writing. But if you care about games, then you should also care about the language available for describing them, and how this language can be corroded by ill-usage.

Take 'awesome,' for example: perhaps the single word that best demonstrates the almost obligatory nature of clichéd language among gamers. Awe is the feeling of active fear and dread, combined with reverence and respect, that's inspired by encountering some great object. Awe is the appropriate emotion of the worshipper who begins to glimpse something divine. It's how the tourist is supposed to feel when visiting supreme natural marvels, such as the Grand Canyon, for the first time – though glossy marketing brochures often diminish the effect by previewing the experience. Wordsworth and other Romantic poets used the term *sublime* to describe a similar effect produced by the Swiss Alps. Witnessing extreme weather events, such as tremendous thunderstorms, at first hand continues to provide us today with opportunities for the kind of holy terror the poets had in mind.

Awe is thus one of our most complex, powerful, mysterious, and sacred emotions, combining pleasure and pain and placing us within the long history of our species upon this planet. Awe is inspired by objects of unmistakable grandeur and authority. We're humbled to the point of feeling afraid for our own insignificance, and at the same time are filled with wonder, adoration, and submissiveness.

By definition, then, nothing smaller than ourselves can ever inspire awe. Yet colloquially 'awesome' is used with just such a weakened meaning: hey, I'm quite impressed. What impresses us about games is a matter of human technology and creativity, rather than forces outside humanity that put us in our cosmic place. Perhaps we no longer recognize the existence of cosmic forces, divine or natural. Alternatively we know these exist but play games in order to hide from them – while we can. Conceivably we mistake game designers and their creations for gods. Has playing videogames ever given you experiences comparable to the holy terror of being outside in a thunderstorm? If not, how might they yet do so?

Sublimity is a measure of the greatest possible effects that individual works of human creativity can produce, and therefore a suitably demanding target for game designers' ambition. By submerging the true meaning of 'awe,' the trivialization enacted through repeated use of 'awesome' actually makes it *more* difficult to discuss how videogames can achieve really high levels of emotional and intellectual power.

You'll say I'm taking this *way* too seriously: at least half of the time 'awesome' is ironic. Exactly – this only proves my point, that gamers seem to feel obliged to continue using this exhausted term for the sake of their social cohesion as a subculture. Clichés are a verbal clinging together against a world of ignorance and potential misunderstanding. To use language without cliché requires not only skill but also courage to step outside and think for yourself.

Deconstruct game hype

The next time a major videogame is about to be launched, arm yourself with some basic knowledge about techniques of propaganda. Is that too strong a word? Surely you can't compare the selling of electronic entertainment products to the Nazis' hateful anti-Semitic campaigns during the 1930s and '40s?

Generally we assume propaganda is bad: outright lies, distortions, and manipulation by an unscrupulous conspiracy with malign intentions. At its worst, propaganda justifies and helps to bring about genocide. Yet Britain and the Allies also used propagandist techniques to help secure the defeat of Hitler's army. Public information films on health and safety likewise attempt persuasion on a mass scale for 'the public good.' They constitute propaganda not because they lie but because they're deliberate, systematic campaigns, designed to produce a particular response from their audience regardless of that audience's wishes.

Pop-up advertisements on the Internet don't first ask, Would you like to see an ad? They literally come right at you and start selling straight away. The game industry is no different from any other manufacturer or service provider in deliberately and systematically using whatever promotional techniques will increase sales and enhance public opinion of their products. Do you think they really care whether players *need* the latest game? Their whole promotional effort goes into producing that impression, whether or not it's true. 'You need this' is the implied tagline of *every* product advertised yesterday, today, and tomorrow. One hopes that company employees, for their own peace of mind, sincerely believe their work helps to improve customers' lives. But this belief can rarely be based on detailed, compassionate, personal knowledge of customers' actual circumstances. When did you last hear any competent salesman voluntarily advise, Well on reflection I really *don't* think you should buy this product, unless it's to say in the next breath, I think you should buy *this* one instead?

None of us likes to believe we're the dupes of advertisers. We prefer to think we'll spot any attempts to influence us and easily shrug them off. The more times you've bought into a sales pitch and then been disappointed, probably the more skeptical you've become. So the next time a major videogame is about to be launched, put your immunity-to-persuasion to a test. The challenge will be greater if it's a game you fully expect to enjoy and therefore find difficult to view objectively.

As a consumer, you've been on the receiving end of marketing hype plenty of times. Gamers know, more or less, what to expect when a new videogame is about to be launched, though advertisers are constantly looking for new tricks. The first previews and demos appear early, via Web sites, magazines, and expos, where you can often meet the developers either in person or through video interviews. Nearer the launch date, there are trailers on the Web, on television, and in cinema, as well as banner, full-page, and hoarding advertisements, all aiming to saturate the market so you can't possibly overlook what's coming. Sign up to the mailing list to receive yet more exclusive previews, demos, breaking news, and developer interviews. On launch night itself, special events run in-store as the queue grows and the clock ticks down. All of these, and more, are designed to produce excitement, anticipation, and an urgent desire to be part of what promises to be an essential experience for every true gamer. Don't miss out!

Appeal to and reinforce the audience's existing beliefs, advises the expert in propaganda techniques (Jowett and O'Donnell's *Propaganda and Persuasion*). Well, the people who make and market videogames are hardly likely to tell gamers they're a bunch of losers. Any salesman knows to flatter the customer: aren't videogames amazing, you gamers are just so cool, you know exactly what you like and recognize quality when you see it, etcetera, etcetera.

Establish yourself as the sole authority and trustworthy expert on the subject at hand. It might seem obvious that game studios should be experts on their own products. That's not the issue. When players trust and are brand-loyal to a particular franchise, developer, or game-related Web site, they know whom to believe when it comes to potentially awkward questions about gaming as a personal habit and cultural phenomenon. What would parents and teachers know?

Establish a monopoly of communication about the subject. For more high-profile launches, studios may tightly control information given to the press. In some cases reviewers are bused to hotels for locked-down preview sessions just days before the launch date.

Target influential opinion-leaders. That'll be the exclusive treatment given to reviewers, and lower down the food-chain to the most loyal players who promote a game for free via fan blogs and Web sites. Keep them happy and they'll spread the news to all their followers in turn.

Use rewards and punishments, the so-called carrot-and-stick treatment. Give 'em exclusives and freebies, and if they cause trouble then (threaten to) ban 'em.

Set up face-to-face meetings with the audience so you can address them directly. Developers routinely give interviews and appear at expos organized and paid for out of the studio's marketing budget. The strategy is to let players feel they know the designers personally, to show how the designers are gamers too and brimming with talent and enthusiasm. It's harder to say no when they're looking you in the eye or when you can put a likeable face to the names.

Engineer crowd situations to encourage a herd mentality. Observe a launch event if you've any doubt about this one. When everyone else itches to get their hands on the new game, surely they can't all be wrong. In the minutes before the doors open, heightened expectation verging on hysteria spreads through the crowd. Moments later and it's a human stampede.

Use visual symbols of power, such as impressive accessories and backdrops. Dictators speak from the steps of monumental buildings draped with giant flags and flanked by uniformed soldiers and officials. Games surround themselves with physically modest but symbolically overblown images of power. Studio logos sizzle with elemental or incendiary force. In-store (point-of-sale) cardboard-cutouts of gun-toting heroes snarl and glare at the player.

Side-Quests and Mini-Games

Use music to stir the audience's emotions. Every videogame has its theme-tune, powerful even before you've played the game and evoking strong memories thereafter. From afar it pulls you toward the game, summoning you to surrender to your fantasies of what it will be like to play.

… So buy me, you know you want to.

The point is not whether you can resist. More difficult is to conceive what would constitute true freedom of choice as a consumer of videogames. Surely it's a fantasy to imagine any gamer capable of adopting a purely objective stance, outside every circuit of persuasion and prior preference. If you're a gamer you're already converted. The same applies to other entertainment media which are heavily promoted and highly popular. It's lonely to stand outside watching *so* many other people apparently having such fun. Don't leave me behind. Yet if we value the idea of freedom we must also have a lurking objection to the powers that hold us enthralled and assume they can count on us.

Pretend you're visiting from Mars

You've arrived with a mission to observe and understand life on Earth, especially that of its dominant species. You come across younger humans engaging in an activity they call *gaming*. Disguised as an Earthling, you set about investigating this phenomenon so as to report back to your fellow Martians, who will hardly believe what you describe.

The challenges of this well-known exercise are to see ourselves as if for the first time and to invent fresh ways of describing what we think we already know. Most importantly, the Martian's observations should be both enlightening and amusing. Their main theme will typically be that human behavior, in this case gaming, is rather bizarre when viewed objectively. Many standup comedians start from a similar assumption when devising material for a routine. There may be elements of social criticism in their observations, pointing to a cynical or pessimistic evaluation of human existence, but overall their aim is to give more pleasure than pain to the audience. The absurdities of our lives can occasion affectionate laughter.

The Martian visitor is a popularized form of the social-science specialism of ethnography. Most commonly, ethnographers adopt the position of *participant observer* in order to gain insights from both inside and outside the field of human culture they're studying. This would mean hanging out with gamers and joining them in multiplayer sessions. Alternatively, *covert naturalistic observation* consists in observing behavior in the natural habitat without being seen. Your task might then be to spot gamers 'in the wild' as in a spoof natural-history program.

What range of activities does this strange thing called 'gaming' consist of? Who counts as a 'gamer,' who doesn't, and what differences in status operate amongst gamers? How does gaming fit into the individual gamer's routine and progression through life-stages? How do gamers themselves describe the origins, meanings, values,

Side-Quests and Mini-Games

and purposes of gaming? How is this different from what non-gamers say and from what you observe to be the reality? Are there any taboos in talking about gaming? What useful function does gaming serve for society over the course of a decade or generation?

Any one of these questions could produce enough observations for an extended field report or comedy routine. All of them require the same initial step: to detach yourself from your habitual point of view. In order to see afresh, you must leave your assumptions behind and become like an innocent. This is easier said than done. Ethnographers have long debated how far it's possible for any individual to step outside personal and cultural frames of reference. Yet it's worth making the attempt. The Martian visitor is one of many devices designed to help us.

Role-play with another gamer, with one of you playing yourself and the other the Martian.

As Martian, ask naïve, childish questions. Deliberately misunderstand. Propose alternative explanations, build an entire theory on a single observation, skew all evidence to fit a particular interpretation, follow an idea to its extreme (absurd) logical conclusion.

Monitor your language for all words and phrases that betray your prior knowledge and experience, such as jargon and insider jokes. Replace these with more literal expressions capturing how you'd describe something if you'd never seen anything like it before.

Laugh at yourself, at your own folly, incompetence, and pomposity. Vent some anger at the worst aspects of game design and gamer behavior. Produce a parody or satire.

Finally, ask yourself how completely we're Earthlings anyway. Some religions (and science fictions) suggest that we are visitors from elsewhere, who have merely grown accustomed to this world and accepted it as reality. When we glimpse gaming as if through the eyes of a complete stranger, is this an opportunity to recognize it as something alien or as in a very deep sense our true home?

Report from the arcade

You can only understand a certain amount about videogames by reflecting on your own experience. The tried-and-tested techniques of documentarists, interviewers, and reporters take you out of yourself and into the wider world of gamers. This world can be delivered to you every day via Web sites and magazines, but that's all secondhand. You can meet and chat in person with plenty of other gamers online, face-to-face, or in shops and arcades, but how often do you adopt the role of documentarist, interviewer, or reporter towards them?

A *documentarist*, typically a film-maker, is concerned to document the discernible facts and reality of particular historical circumstances and lived experiences, especially those which are misunderstood, ignored, politically sensitive, or about to be lost to human memory. How might these categories apply to the world of gaming? Which aspects of contemporary gaming culture are worth documenting, and how much of this work currently goes on?

An *interviewer* is skilled in using dialogue to tease interesting speech from individuals selected for their expertise, representativeness, popularity, or newsworthiness. More often than not, the person interviewed by game journalists is someone in the industry, typically in the design and development team. What other kinds of people are involved in gaming as a cultural phenomenon, and what unique perspectives might they have to offer?

A *reporter* must arrive at his or her own understanding of a situation and then summarize this in a concise, insightful, informative, and engaging way for the benefit of an audience. This task comes closest to the existing role of the game journalist who reports on industry news and events, or of journalists specializing in other fields (such as media, education, technology, or society) reporting on how videogames intrude on their patch. How much of the wider world of gaming goes unreported? How do different audiences each receive a report biased towards their interests?

Common to these three disciplines are the journalist's core values of curiosity, truthfulness, and objectivity. These aren't absolute. Documentaries may foreground the subjective perceptions of the film-maker, for example, and a reporter may question the possibility of arriving at any definitive version of the truth. Indeed, as part of any enquiry the enquirers must now and then pause to ask themselves what they're doing and why. But on this occasion, as a contrast to your usual personal experience, you'll mostly want to focus externally on the facts and reality of what you encounter more than internally on your perceptions and responses. Just for today, other gamers' experience will be what counts, rather than your own. Empathy and interpretation will be important, but so will objectivity and accuracy.

Ethically, you'll need to respect privacy and confidentiality, for example by ensuring anonymity or gaining informed consent. As an observer of gamers at play, your voyeurism should be discrete, non-intimidating, and non-coercive (in other words, not subtly maneuvering a person in ways they might later regret).

Mentally don the journalist's traditional raincoat and shoulder-bag. Take up your camera, microphone, and notebook. First, find your subject. This may be a person or a place, someone or somewhere that you know well or have never visited. Time your visit according to when your hoped-for action or characters are likely to appear. Lurk, ask around, peek behind the scenes, keep watch until you find what or whom you're looking for, which you may not recognize until that moment. Maybe it's something special, or appears rather ordinary.

What you're looking for will be like a reflection of yourself in the mirror – an aspect of your past, what you'd love to become, or what you most loathe and fear – or a strange vision of how gaming can include such very different people and experiences from the world you usually inhabit.

Once you've found your subject, your next task is to gather and record information through whatever means are to hand. Whether you're at an arcade, game shop, or tournament, are watching gamers in a park, on public transport, or in an online multiplayer game, practice your observation skills. Look more closely than usual, even if you're able to take photographs or screenshots, as if in preparation for a memory test.

Like Sherlock Holmes, what details can you notice which give clues to character? What's the story behind appearances? Focus on facts first, rather than leap too quickly to speculation. So far as possible, remain nonjudgmental. Regardless of your personal opinion, what must it be like to participate in that gaming scene, to occupy the skin of that gamer? Imagine you're the eyes and ears of someone unable to witness this scene in person, for whose benefit your task is above all to describe, or like a recording machine save the scene faithfully for future recall.

Possibly you'll enter conversation, spoken or typed. Hope they'll talk, and say interesting things! If not, it's up to you to ask questions or make comments that will get the conversation flowing. You might try a direct approach or subtlety, flattery or confrontation. Standard advice is to gain the person's trust so they'll confide; you can do this through honesty or cunning. At the very least you must show curiosity, since boredom will turn both of you off.

Genuine dialogue, enabling a meeting of minds which would otherwise remain more-or-less confined to their own skulls, should always be a risky, thrilling, and potentially life-changing encounter. You or your interviewee might not be ready for this, and often the contact seems to occur more accidentally than deliberately.

Should you proceed to produce a report, drawing on what you've learnt through your observations and conversations, your attention must now switch in part to your audience, whoever that may be. Without one you *can't* report. Nor can your audience be too close to your subject, since they'll then already know too much about it, in which case your report will really be a form of commentary. A reporter, by contrast, acts as a go-between bridging a gap in knowledge and personal experience that otherwise exists between audience and subject. That means either between gamers and non-gamers or across some of the major divides among different kinds of gamer.

Your next problem will then be to find channels of communication. These different groups necessarily don't talk to each other much. Like a peacemaker – unfortunately gamers are in some ways besieged by and in dispute with the wider culture – you must find common ground where both sides may meet.

Enter the world of stick-people

You've met them on street signs and toilet doors. They're a minimum representation of a person, with head, body, arms, and legs drawn cleverly to communicate an array of scenarios. Older stick-people walk leaning forwards from the waist and with a stick in one hand. Electrocuted stick-person is attacked by arrow-headed, zigzag lightning.

From an efficient device in graphic communication, stick-people have entered popular culture through humorous comic strips, pop-art and, more recently, their own subgenre of casual videogames. Because of his lack of defining features, stick-man typically represents an everyman character, who may be put-upon by the world or heroic despite his ordinariness. I say stick-man because he's often called that and in videogames acquires by association some of the attributes of other game heroes, who are mostly male. Also, the signs on toilet doors stereotype stick-women as skirt-wearers, however many of the women and girls entering wear trousers.

Stick-man is silhouette-black and naked apart from an occasional bandanna. We neither see nor miss his genitalia, nor his muscles, nor his military camouflage outfit, all of which are markers of masculine power. His gun is often equally stick-like. He's of no particular race, creed, or nationality, unless otherwise identified through accompanying text or images.

He's what all those macho videogame heroes would be if stripped of their visual glitz, namely a cursor function. He's the player's point of action within the game. In early prototypes, developers might work with just such a simplified icon, or wireframe model, to represent the player, since this is all that's required in order to test the basic functionality of movement and interaction with objects in the game's space. Character- and set-dressing come later.

Some players have little interest in the dressing. They know that the game's underlying algorithm, determining what happens in the game and defining what you must do to win, ignores much of the surface appearance designed to immerse the player in the game's fictional world. If you're hit, it doesn't matter whether your hair is long or short, dark or blonde, straight or curly. Cover is cover whether it's textured to look like a crate, a barrel, or a rock. In fact this understanding comes to all of us in those situations where we end up replaying a sequence over and over in order to figure out how to complete it successfully. When you've died at the same spot ten times in a row, you no longer care what it or your character looks like. You just want to know the precise combination and timing of actions that will enable you to progress. At this point you might as well be a stick-person in a stick-world. It's often at this level that testers identify functional flaws in a game's design or programming.

Don't be fooled that games with a stick-aesthetic must therefore lack emotional punch. No full-length mainstream videogame, movie, or animation has yet featured a stick-person as its hero. That's more likely to happen in student exercises by allowing practice in basic design principles without the need for intensive graphics. Yet stick-people can have a uniquely powerful everyman appeal. The magic of artists and writers can make us care surprisingly much about their little triumphs and give them a distinctive personality.

Stick-bodies, such as that of the animated modeling-clay character, Morph, from Tony Hart's British children's television series, can be made to shape-shift in exaggerated ways impossible for more realistic characters. This morphing can be a joyful exercising of powers that we humans would like to possess, or a visual metaphor of pain. We assume that stick-bodies basically resemble ours – when they're shot they spurt blood – yet they can also be more elastic and sprightly, more resilient or fragile. This applies to all cartoon characters, but with stick-people it's immediately apparent. Bodies comprising nothing but lines can obviously transform in any way a line can, by stretching, turning corners, becoming dashed, fattening, changing color, and so on.

Imagining and giving meaning to a mobile world composed entirely of lines is the special skill of animators. It's partly an extension of how children think when they draw. In a wax-crayon world – depicted in casual videogames such as *Doodle Jump* – individual identity and relationships between things are rather different from in the adult world. There are houses and flowers, cars and stars, mummies and daddies, but not really any individuals. Visual resemblance is less important than essential identity. Objects interact magically more than by the laws of physics.

The faces drawn by children, comprising a circle with two dots for the eyes and a line for the mouth, illustrate how basic a pattern can be for us to recognize it as something especially important for us. Cartoonists know that apparently simplistic, so-called iconic drawings of faces can convey intense emotion. A 'smiley' may represent anyone because it's empty of any signs of individuality. Viewers therefore identify with the face more easily and fill it with their own emotion – more so than if the face represented a particular person smiling.

In short, stick-world is psychologically expressive and potentially fertile territory for videogames as they diversify in their use of visual styles.

a. Choose an existing 3D videogame and imagine, if you can, what it might be like when stripped back to a stick-world. Once the visual dressing is removed, what essential gameplay remains?

b. Practice viewing the world around you in stick-mode. That's stick-football those stick-kids are playing, and stick-coffee the stick-waiter is serving inside the stick-café. In various situations, how might you visually express people's emotions through stick-characters?

c. Consider what happens when worlds collide. What adventures await black-and-white stick-people when they find themselves in the multicolored real world that you inhabit or in the graphically-realistic world of a three-dimensional videogame? And how would you or that 3D game's characters fare when transported into a flat, black-and-white stick-world?

Analogize a digital game

Choose any videogame that you know sufficiently well that you can recall, or visualize in your mind's eye, a typical sequence of play. This might feature running across rooftops, say, or dragging cards into suits, or driving through city streets, or scoring from a free kick, or directing your troops to attack an enemy base. You might imagine this action taking place on a screen, as when you played it, or happening around you, as if you're inside the world of the game.

Now select some basic elements of this sequence and try to visualize them reproduced *mechanically*, as in an old-fashioned amusement arcade, fairground, or carnival. Objects are now made of painted metal, carved wood, molded plastic, printed cardboard, stitched leather, and stuffed cloth. They move on cogs, springs, and ratchets – you don't know how exactly, as you're out front enjoying the show.

Recall, if you know it, the derby racing game where a row of players sits frenziedly aiming balls into colored hoops to score points that jerk their horse, camel, dolphin, or reindeer from right to left. Whoever's the first to reach the far side wins. The mechanical version of the game you're imagining is more sophisticated than that. All its workings are concealed and smooth-gliding, ticking and whirring quietly as in the heyday of automata, when clockwork dolls and animals amazed the royalty of Europe with their lifelike behavior: little miracles of ingenuity, engineering, and illusion.

The scenery is mostly flats, like in a toy theater. (It might help to think of the two-dimensionality revived in *Paper Mario* and *LittleBigPlanet*.) Objects in the distance are miniatures placed only a few yards away. Instead of a gamepad or other controller familiar from today's systems, you work at levers, knobs, and wheels which transmit your physical force directly to the objects on stage. Sound effects are supplied by horns, whistles, drums, bells, and rattles. The special effects belong to Victorian theater: jets of flame, billows of dry ice, tricks with mirrors. Characters pop up from trapdoors in the floor or descend on wires as if from the skies. A canvas backdrop falls to convey a change of scene, or scrolls as you move sideways. Yet they've also found a way to simulate three-dimensional space by allowing you to swivel the stage in the direction you wish to look and having objects move on tracks from the back of the stage towards you, somehow growing larger as they come.

Whoever worked out the precise mechanisms and all their interactions must be a genius. Yet you're beginning to address some conceptual problems just by imagining what effects the game might aim to achieve.

Say *Legend of Zelda*'s elf-like Link has become a complexly-jointed cutout puppet. When you turn him right or left, his limbs flick nimbly on unseen pivots, and the tail of his green cap quivers. When he jumps, you glimpse the titanium upright supporting him from below. When he strikes with his sword, little red shards ray from the blade to imitate blood-spurt. When he swims, a veil of shimmering turquoise fabric drops in front of the stage, wafting wave-like in a side-draft. When he reaches the end of a level, he gives you a mechanical smile over his shoulder. When he dies, an ocarina melody haunts offstage.

There's a genre of science fiction, called steampunk, that undertakes a similar kind of imaginative experiment. Typically it goes back to a prior period in human history, such as the pre-electric steam-age of the nineteenth century, and soups up the technology of the day to achieve by alternative means something like what we have now, or even what we might conceive for the future.

Many of today's videogames derive from yesterday's analog originals. Simulations of card games, such as Solitaire, are an obvious example. In the prehistory of videogames, alongside sports, playground games, and board games we find amusement arcades and theme parks. Rollercoaster rides, pinball cabinets, and shooting galleries all developed as popular entertainments in the late nineteenth century. They did mechanically much of what videogames now do digitally. We usually consider this transition from analog to digital to constitute the forward direction of 'progress,' partly because videogames can so quickly and cheaply bring such a wide variety of amusements to so many individual homes, and partly because they can do things their originals couldn't.

Yet the technical challenge of designing and constructing a mechanical *Legend of Zelda* remains ahead of us, in a potential future. Even as a one-off princely folly or international inventors' challenge, how far could we go in recreating a videogame mechanically?

Aesthetically – in terms of the artistic and sensory pleasures they give – who's to say that analogized versions of digital games won't become a future trend? Human beings are, for the foreseeable future, creatures who delight in touch and the uniqueness of material objects in time and place. This is something more than nostalgia for childhood toys, though that's partly responsible for the success of *LittleBigPlanet*, with its tactile simulations of wood, cloth, string, paper, and cardboard. Their simulated textures won't age with us, whereas the green of mechanical Link's cap has gradually faded from the beating of the sun. In his original digital worlds, by contrast, Link remains eternally young, safe from the wear of time – yet also dated by the graphics of his day.

Part of the pleasure of playing today's videogames is seeing how well they can simulate different environments in terms of visual appearance, ambient sounds, and behavior of objects. In some ways, it doesn't really matter what the game's about, since what really interests us is what this technology can now do. No analog gaming system yet exists of sufficient capability to provide an alternative to today's digital systems – of consoles, motion-sensitive controllers, flat-screens, surround-sound, and so on. If it did, I expect most gamers would at least try it out. The question is still worth asking: *is it the game you love or the digital gaming system?* Is it the song that you love whatever instrument it's played on, or the instrument whatever tune it's playing?

Co-play a single-player game

Arrange a mirror so you can see within it whatever screen you're playing on – typically a television, handheld device, or computer monitor. Now look into the mirror and try to play the game back-to-front (reversed left-to-right).

Alternatively, try playing upside-down. Turn the controller, keyboard, or handheld around by 180 degrees, so you hold it upside-down. Or do the same with the television or computer screen, if that's possible, so that the picture is upside-down.

Persevere and you'll eventually begin to move beyond the initial disorientation which, depending on the game, should set a fresh challenge even for expert players. This experiment recalls those in optical transformations of perception first undertaken in the 1890s. Test subjects wearing spectacles with lenses designed to flip the image upside-down gradually became accustomed to the new configuration and perceived it as normal – after a lot of giddy-drunken falling-about, obviously. How long does it take you, when playing back-to-front or upside-down, to begin regaining some of your usual skill? How do things start to piece together after the initial perceptual breakdown?

For an aural version of this challenge, sit next to someone who's playing a different game from you and swap headphones so that you're listening to the wrong soundtrack. Depending on the game pairings you should notice some interesting interference. In this case your disorientation will be cognitive as well as perceptual. *That* sound doesn't fit with *that* action.

In effect you're performing your own sabotage of the game. Retro/arcade game sabotages are a recent sub-genre of casual games, and many other videogames contain moments of deliberately-induced disorientation, when the controls start operating not quite as they should. Suddenly it's as if you're drunk, or the boat's pitching violently, and you can't walk straight.

Side-Quests and Mini-Games

There are potentially similar elements of disorientation in the following exercise, but they're only part of it.

Choose a single-player game and arrange yourself and a partner comfortably so that you can *both* take hold of the *same* set of controls. For example, the player sitting on the left takes hold of the right side of the gamepad with her right hand, while the player sitting on the right takes hold of the left side with her left hand. For a computer game, one player might take charge of the mouse and the other the keyboard, or you could split use of the keyboard.

Alternatively, have player A turn their back to play blind with the help of player B's running commentary.

Videogames have already explored aspects of cooperative play. Usually this entails two or more players each with their own controls and character, playing as a team. On home consoles, the screen is often split to show what each player is doing. On networked consoles, handhelds, or PCs, each player has their own screen. In either case, whether directly in the same room or via in-game chat (spoken using headsets or typed), players must communicate verbally to coordinate joint action. Multiplayer modes have become increasingly popular because of this social dimension, and developers now routinely design even single-player games with this extension in mind.

More rarely, control of a single character is split between players. A simple example appeared in an early version of the arcade classic *Space Invaders* for the Atari home console. The console came with two very basic controllers, each comprising a joystick and single red button. In variants of the main *Space Invaders* game, player A could move the cannon only to the left and player B move it only to the right, or one player could only move and the other only shoot.

You can impose similar constraints on today's gaming systems in the manner described above. The greater complexity of today's systems means that more interesting things are liable to happen as you divide up the controls between the players. This will vary depending on which controls you choose to allocate to each player, what actions the particular game allows you to perform, and how these are mapped to the controls.

For example, one common configuration of controls in a console game is for the left hand to control movement, camera, and targeting via joystick and directional buttons, while the right hand controls attacks, blocks, and other actions via colored buttons. In this case, you might find it fairly easy to play the game with the help of running commentary, as you give each other instructions or explain what you intend to do. Alternatively you'll come across specific knots, where confusion sets in and you can't act as smoothly as normal. Under the heat of enemy fire, you don't have sufficient time to verbalize your decision-making process and die more quickly than usual. Faced with a tricky jump, you're unable to coordinate the use of multiple controls across both hands and keep falling. Trying to turn a series of corners, you begin to feel nauseous as the direction you move and the direction you look become discoordinated.

Notice what becomes difficult in the particular situation you devise. If you stick with it, how are you able to improve? If possible, divide up the controls differently and play again. At least swap sides so you get to try the other half of the controls, or take turns to commentate.

How is the experience different if you co-play with someone of a similar ability to your own or with someone who's a much better or worse player? Or with someone who's better or worse at leading, communicating, or following instructions?

What's frustrating and what's pleasurable in working with your partner in this way, more intimately than you'd do in other co-op games? Where are your personal limits in the amount of control you require in order to enjoy the gaming experience?

The street-theater company Royal de Luxe produces wondrous spectacles with their giant mechanical figures crewed by large teams of puppeteers. The Sultan's Elephant, for example, comparable in scale to one of the Colossi in *Shadows of the Colussus*, enchanted Londoners in 2006 with its magnificent, benign presence. How might videogames build in cooperative play by featuring giant characters that require a crew of multiple players in order to operate?

Go gray

The average age of gamers is currently estimated to be in the mid-thirties and rising every year. This means that, given the large number of teenage players, there must also be quite a few gray-haired gamers. Thankfully, perhaps, designers have not yet created games quite as narrowly gray as Barbie dolls are definitively pink. There's *Brain Trainer* – advertised using models flatteringly younger than the target market – but not yet games centered on Zimmer frames and crochet. Maybe it's only a matter of time before *Care-Home Breakout*, complete with senile zombies and nurse-manager bosses. Surely designers will not limit themselves to such crass game concepts if the average age of gamers eventually reaches the mid-fifties.

Enjoying improved longevity, good health, prosperity, and liberal social attitudes, generations of sky-diving grandmothers and night-clubbing grandfathers challenge stereotypes about older people. Life now begins not at forty but at sixty. Yet among videogame heroes there's barely a gray hair to be seen – older Snake in *Metal Gear Solid 4: Guns of the Patriots* being a notable exception. Unless they simply cannot imagine anything different, commercial developers (including some lead-designers and studio executives who are themselves in midlife, having begun their careers as pioneers in the early days of gaming) must assume their core market will reject any player-character who doesn't visibly radiate youthful vigor. After all, that's what's done by a thousand other faces smiling in music videos, fashion advertisements, and television shows. A large proportion of popular entertainment is built around teenagers and twenty-somethings, who form a constantly-renewed mass of cultural consumers eager to see themselves reflected onscreen.

Beauty and grooming products, cosmetic surgery, and fitness centres promise that, with enough effort, we can all prolong our stay in the youth club. Like Super Mario, James Bond, or Cher, we too can look like we haven't aged a day in decades. This is a pleasant fantasy but only a fraction of the entire drama of a whole life, which ultimately forms the range of subject matter for any creative medium.

Even if videogames in future might better reflect their increasingly aging audience, for the moment there remain generational divides among gamers. We can characterize these in very broad terms as follows.

Younger gamers have grown up with digital technologies as everyday tools for work and play. You are the so-called digital natives. Ever since you've known them, videogames have been a relatively established medium. Many of your most formative experiences happened while you were at the keyboard or controls.

By contrast, midlife gamers, such as those my age, knew nothing of computers when we started out and have incorporated them into our working and leisure lives as we've gone along. We are digital immigrants. When I was a teenager living in a small British seaside town during the early 1980s, videogames were considerably more basic than today. No coin-operated arcade classic could provide as richly formative experiences as the PC and console games released even a decade later.

As for my parents' generation, digital technologies – whether personal computers, mobile telephones, digital cameras, MP3 players, or videogames – have entered their lives even later, typically in retirement, and therefore in a more patchy way. For many of this age group, the land of digital technologies remains a foreign country. Older gamers are thus a minority among their own generation (and of course among the population of gamers as a whole) in a way that doesn't apply to younger and midlife gamers, and that may gradually cease to apply as midlife gamers themselves become elders.

One day you, too, will be old enough to sit quietly with a blanket over your knees while you watch the children play. Will you still be gaming? Assuming that gaming may have become something very different by then, what will be the videogames of your past – such as those you're playing today – that you'll treasure? It may be that you'll have difficulty replaying them, since the latest-generation console you bought recently, joining a club of millions, will by then have become antique. In your memory the games of your youth will be keys to an entire lost world of joy and sorrow. How will you begin to reply when a child, wizard in the new-fangled gaming of her age, takes the souvenir from your knotted hands and asks, *what is this?*

    a. Identify some stereotypes of middle-aged or older people and subvert these so as to imagine unconventional game characters and game-worlds they can inhabit as heroes. Alternatively, choose an existing videogame character and imagine the exploits they'll undertake in their senior years.

    b. Find out what it was like to be young in decades past. What distinctive experiences – not limited to those popularized in nostalgic clichés of the mid-twentieth century – did children and teenagers have in the past that could form the basis of a videogame?

    c. Use gaming as a means to initiate or enrich a cross-generational relationship.

EPILOGUE

Epilogue

Gaming's highest ideals

Outside the law court stands the goddess Justice, also known as Themis, sword in one hand, scales in the other, and sometimes blindfolded to show her impartiality. The city is London, or Brasilia, or Frankfurt, or Memphis, or Brisbane, or Hong Kong. She was placed there by modern hands. As adornment? Not merely. She represents the highest principles that should govern the proceedings within. Secular rationalists do not believe the statue represents any real, supernatural being with magical power to affect what happens in this world. Instead her image functions symbolically by personifying ideals in a memorable human form, in a similar way to a role-model.

Lady Justice is what's called a *tutelary deity*, supposedly acting as tutor to all those who work in the legal profession, especially judges. She gives hope to plaintiffs, defendants, and witnesses who pass within the walls of the court that justice will truly be done therein. The need for a personification of Justice is strong enough for her statue to reappear around the world. Fallible, vulnerable human beings, whether religious believers or not, need inspirational images such as these to remind them of sustaining values and reassure them of the possibility of a better future.

What are the highest ideals of videogame developers, critics, educators, and players? This question matters if we assume that gamers, standing on the shoulders of all previous generations, in some way hold the promise of a better future for humankind. What are the darkest hours when someone involved with gaming might seek a personified ideal to call upon for help? Can we adapt existing symbolic figures for the purpose, or do we need to create new ones?

Consider the function of *patron saints* – originally a religious term but now used more broadly. Catholicism recognizes hundreds of these angelic ex-humans, whose purpose is to intercede with God on humanity's behalf to seek answers to its prayers in times of need, either one's own or others'. The saint acts as patron (champion, spokesperson, and sponsor) for particular aspects of life, including occupations and activities, with which she or he was associated as an historical person. It takes centuries for the Church to recognize new saints, but in principle there's a saint for every occasion, even the most modern. Thus a Catholic astronaut might carry an image of St. Christopher, patron saint of travelers, since the historical Christopher allegedly carried people safely across a dangerous river.

In popular usage of the term, any famous person can potentially become the patron saint of their particular field. Nominations for videogaming's patron saint might include its pioneers and leading figures who devoted their lives to the cause. To adapt the Catholic Church's criteria for recognition as a saint (canonization), we'd require candidates for gaming's patron saint to – metaphorically at least – be dead, have lived an exemplary life, and either have been martyred or have performed miracles. These achievements testify to the person's elevation to the heaven of gaming and closeness to its divinity, however we might imagine those.

Muses, on the other hand, are sources of creative inspiration. Strictly speaking, Greek mythology recognized only nine of these goddess-like figures. They were patrons of the forms of art and literature, such as lyric poetry and tragic drama, that existed and were highly regarded in ancient times. The muse herself (always female) spoke or played through the human individual, who served merely as a medium.

Members of a game development team, if so inclined, would each need to approach a muse appropriate for their creative specialism. Her image might watch discretely from a corner of their workspace, say.

Players, too, can be creative as performers in some games. Might Terpsichore, muse of dancing, inspire great players of rhythm games?

Within the fictional world of a videogame, any number of deities, saints, or muses might be appropriate to call upon, depending on the kinds of place and activity being simulated: defending a city, navigating booby-trapped terrain, charming the villagers with your lute playing, and so on. I wonder, though, whether these would instead all come under the patronage of a single, more general personification, namely the ideal gamer, who inspires you to play beyond your abilities whatever the game.

Videogames incorporate an eclectic variety of mythical, legendary, and supernatural beings from around the world in their storylines and characters. Often these are misappropriated, in other words taken out of their original cultural context and blithely reinvented for the purposes of the game's fantasy. Any real power of ideals they originally embodied then tends to be lost. In action-adventure games, for example, abandoned temples styled as ancient Egyptian, Buddhist, or Aztec serve as little more than picturesque climbing frames. The power of a whole people's centuries-long worship is supposedly downloaded into a single magical relic which the greedy try to remove. This is the myth of the Holy Grail, among others. Videogame stories and imagery thus testify to our continuing hunger for mythological and spiritual meaning.

In role-playing games the *priest* is a staple character class, typically skilled in healing and protection rather than attack. In the real world this term is usually restricted to religious contexts, but metaphorically has wider application. Priests guard and mediate the power of high ideals and sacred images within any particular field. To become a secular priest or priestess of gaming, whether as a player, developer, critic, or educator, you'll need to give up any ideas of possessing special powers for yourself. That way lies corruption, as we know from cartoonish stories of evil, power-hungry high priests. Your service must be selfless and devoted to the best interests of gaming and gamers.

In any church, the ratio of priests to congregation is low. Few are those called to the ministry. Fewer still are those mystics and theologians who formulate our understanding of the holy and evolve it over time.

As the judge embodies the Law, so you'll embody Gaming in your very person. Where the judge wears a wig and gown, what might you wear as the uniform of your office? Where the judge sits in court, what is gaming's temple? Where the judge bows before the figure of Justice, whose image will you set up to honor? As the judge's loyalty is twofold – to the Law and to humans passing before the bench – so will you serve both the ideals of gaming and those who apply to them in time of need.

These final few missions consider what philosophers call teleological matters, in other words the endpoints and ultimate purposes of any activity.

Epilogue

Monitor gamers in the media

You already know the negative, anti-gamerist stereotypes. Allegedly gamers are obese couch-potatoes, red-eyed and unhygienic. They're nerdy geeks incapable of ordinary conversation. They're time-wasting, work-shy underachievers. They're greasy, sloppily-dressed adolescents aged twelve to forty. They're latent school-killers brainwashed by violent fantasies.

You recognize these clichés from the media. A politician speaks earnestly on television, a newspaper headline reveals academic research, a poster campaign features a boy entranced… Sometimes explicitly, sometimes more subtly and by implication, and not always in clichés, we're told what gamers are like. We can also see for ourselves, from the reflection in the mirror, from gamers we know personally, from customers walking into a local game retail store, from people spotted playing on handhelds in the park.

Some of the clichés contain a fair amount of truth, others hardly any. That applies to all stereotypes – shorthand representations – whatever the social group. What matters is how stereotypes can lead to harmful consequences for the particular group. Gamers often receive bad press that we might assume at the least encourages dismissive, suspicious, and hostile attitudes towards them from some non-gamers.

It's not all bad news, however. Gamers are also portrayed in the media as being techno- and future-savvy and thus in some way pioneers ahead of their time. Apparently they're already at home in the virtual worlds that will one day, it seems, encompass all work and leisure. With their arcane knowledge, nimble fingers, and lightning-fast reactions, they're its action heroes in-waiting. Cool.

All of these figures, both positive and negative, shape gamers' own self-image. They're versions of themselves to live up to, to blank out, to challenge, or to foster. This is only partly a conscious, rational, and well-informed process. By systematically monitoring how gamers appear in the media, you can become more aware of what images are available and the emotional and persuasive power attaching to them – as figures of hope or fear, desire or loathing, benediction or cursing. Is it also possible to determine how far each image actually has a basis in truth?

The various images of gamers serve different interest groups. Gamers' appearance in the public imagination is influenced by journalists, PR agents for the game industry, lobbyists for various interest groups, academics, and gamers themselves. Each seeks to pull public perceptions in its favor. Gamers are disadvantaged in this contest by lacking a clear institutional voice, speaking on their behalf with the authority of a representative organization.

You might nevertheless try to become an icon-maker or image-shaper yourself. Stereotypes don't disappear overnight, vanishing with a pop into nothingness. They either gradually fade or are actively transformed, for example through creative or humorous intervention. In that case, you should ask yourself which images of gamers best serve your own purposes. For that matter, what purposes *do* you have regarding how gamers are perceived, both by themselves and by the wider public? Do you wish gamers would just be seen differently or actually be different? If you happened to become a media mogul in a position to influence public opinion, what social status, powers, and responsibilities would you choose to attribute to gamers?

Epilogue

Name that learning

For a long while educators feared that videogames taught little or nothing of value and distracted pupils from their proper studies. Some anti-videogame lobbyists went further and argued that shooters, in particular, trained players to become killers. Today, many organizations recognize how well people of all ages can learn by playing. They've therefore begun to make games, whether a humble quiz, a purpose-designed videogame, or a learning 'quest' structured into a series of missions, more central to their training and educational strategies.

The basic principle is that games can make learning fun and therefore more successful. Some educationalists go so far as to argue that play is in fact our single *best* model of learning, and that classroom activities should therefore be redesigned around games as *much* as possible, not as little. On this thinking, students might be most at risk of failing to learn whenever they're *not* playing – so long as their play has been designed for teaching purposes.

Gaming constitutes a new kind of literacy. Not only are videogames, in all their variety, an increasingly common point of reference shared amongst peer groups and across generations, but the worlds of work, social interaction, and politics have become more game-like and young people need the experience of complex, structured play as an essential preparation for the life ahead of them.

Generally it's easier to recognize as being 'educational' certain types of approved content that have been given a game-style presentation. Less familiar and easy to articulate are the educational qualities of gaming and play as activities regardless of, or in addition to, the content. Yet we understand this when children are told to 'go and play.' What they play matters, but so does the mere act of playing, which is deemed to be good in itself. Likewise a music teacher may have some preferred pieces for her pupils to practice, but *any* piece will also do. At an elementary level, schoolchildren are required to read at least some literature and perform at least a handful of scientific experiments, less for the specific lessons they'll learn than for the mere exposure to certain ways of relating to the world that are fundamental to human culture.

Instead of teaching mindlessly violent and aggressive behavior, as might superficially appear, a multiplayer shooting game may actually teach cooperation, strategic thinking, teamwork, and communication skills, in so far as these are required in order to be able to succeed at the game. On a case by case basis, what kinds of learning are made possible by playing particular games in particular situations and over a period of time? To answer this, you might consider some of the following questions.

In what varieties of social interaction does the game encourage players to engage? What social skills and patterns of behavior are involved? How does the game present a world of freedoms and constraints, of choices and consequences? How does it foster individuality and how does it promote collective thinking and behavior?

How does the game present structured challenges in the development and use of generic (transferable) skills, such as puzzle solving? How does the game excite in players a desire to achieve, a willingness to persevere, courage to take calculated risks, and confidence in their abilities?

How must players make meaning out of complex or uncertain situations in the game? How does the game produce an engaging emotional drama or intellectual journey? Does it prompt the player to consider any significant ethical or political issues? How does the player distinguish between the world of the game and the real world, and also make connections between these? In what kinds of thoughtful discussion do players engage after playing the game?

How might the game be designed differently so as to lead to a different answer to any of the above?

All of these questions prepare for larger ones that are of greater ultimate concern. Can we say what sort of person gaming helps to produce – what type of mind and body, what kind of friend, partner, colleague, and citizen? What virtues of character does it foster, what expertise of benefit to society, and what forces for good in the world? Though hard to measure even for established academic subjects and teaching methods, such are the traditional endpoints of education, and such must be those of learning based around games.

Remember the electronic graveyard

What human hands actually made that game console on which you play, and from where did the raw materials come? That scratched disk you threw in the bin, that old laptop you part-exchanged, where exactly did they end their days? Ethical consumerism and e-waste recycling – I feel a rant coming on, spoiling your fun again.

It seems that competitive pricing requires meagerly-paid and strictly-disciplined factory workers, that upgrade culture demands the plundering of natural materials and the piling-up of noxious scrap-heaps. Impossible, at least for now, to have one without the other. We don't have to face this fact, however, since the unpleasantness of electronics manufacturing and waste disposal are conveniently shunted away from our doorsteps to industrial areas on the other side of town or the other side of the world.

Perhaps the horror stories are exaggerated, of exploitation, despoliation, and pollution. Companies in all sectors of the electronics industry would presumably like you to believe this, and preferably for you not to hear the stories in the first place, since that makes life easier for them. 'Social responsibility' and 'corporate ethics' are now standard buzzwords of the public-relations image many companies construct for themselves, with varying degrees of sincerity.

But you sell your old games and consoles via online auction, or trade them at local game exchanges, right? At best this merely disguises or defers the problem. Raw materials are still required for making new – assuming you still intend to keep up with at least some of the latest games – and most of what you passed on will eventually end up in an incinerator, dump, or landfill, imperfectly recycled.

Games aren't much different from other types of consumer electronics in this respect. Worry too much and you'll never again buy a new digital camera, flat-screen television, or mobile telephone. Refuse to buy new and you're still implicated, as you just get someone else to do the dirty-work of buying new for you while you wait to rescue their cast-offs. Opt out altogether, then, and where will it stop – rags for underwear, dry bread and water for supper? At least recycling old games is better than nothing.

Maybe so, yet how many gamers are really prepared to make do with the old? What kind of gamer are you if you don't at least hanker after the latest-generation hardware and releases? Retro-gaming is an established scene, celebrating older games and systems, but even this offers relatively minor opposition to the dominant upgrade culture. From the frenzy of high-profile launches, you might imagine that supporting the onward march of videogames resembles a holy duty, overriding anything so petty as ecological concerns. Like the drive to put men on the moon, what's at stake is apparently humankind's destiny to reach ever higher achievements in the sphere of entertainment. Only in this case it's not just a handful of carefully-selected men who'll defy gravity and escape earth's orbit. Every gamer, seemingly, deserves to be part of the great adventure, justifying millions of individual engines for leaping into ever-more thrilling virtual worlds.

In its extreme form, this imaginary flight to the electronic heavens has been called techno-transcendentalism. What it seeks to transcend is the physical Earth and the individual body where we must each live. Both are abandoned as cradles that have been outgrown, or as graveyards for those not brave enough to make the leap into the future. The cyber-astronaut, placing his faith in the latest high-tech consumer electronics, leaves the land and flesh behind as so many broken dreams of a paradise to be found only in a digital body moving in digital space. In a vivid phrase, the body is viewed as 'meat,' tiresomely demanding to be fed, cleaned, rested, and clothed. Rainforests, oceans, and polar icecaps, meanwhile, can all be trashed so long as their digital simulations become ever-more complete. Take whatever's needed in order to get out of here.

To continue the spaceflight analogy, what goes up must come down. There's nowhere else to go, as yet. The Earth is our home for the foreseeable future, as is the physical body during this lifetime. Unless a hero's welcome awaits, cyber-astronauts crash-land, or burn up on reentering the atmosphere, or fall as debris from a stratospheric explosion. Safely returned, they must walk once more the ordinary world they thought to leave behind for good. Like one reborn, perhaps they'll find it more beautiful and precious.

How far, if at all, does this caricature reflect your own experience of gaming? Consider the realities of your actions as well as the psychological accuracy of the analogy. For example, the surest way to reduce e-waste is to reduce production in the first place, so that no recycling is required. Would you consider actively resisting the upgrade culture, perhaps by boycotting new consoles? Would you pay higher prices for your gaming experience if you knew the extra revenue would go towards improving the wages of workers in electronics factories, as in a Fair Trade scheme, or towards ecological conservation programs? How many gamers want to know the back-story of game production and disposal – their social, economic, and environmental realities – and are you one of them?

Epilogue

End cut-scene

EXT. GAMER GATES
Wireless game controller in hand, PLAYER rises from the couch and stands awestruck before a set of monumental gates. Their titanic heights part-shrouded in swirling mist, the gates seem alive with iconic videogame characters, leaping and posing for combat, winking and snarling. All else around PLAYER is blank: the couch has disappeared, and there's nowhere else to go.

> (as if recorded message)
> Roll up, roll up! Points mean prizes! Do we have a winner? Only the greatest champions admitted, no losers here thank you. Come on if you think you've got what it takes. This way please.

GATEKEEPER is suddenly beside PLAYER. He's bizarrely outfitted and equipped as if just come from a cosplay convention where the aim was to play several characters at once. On one foot he wears a gladiator's sandal, on the other a footballer's boot. Over torn jeans are strapped ornate metal shin guards and pistol holsters. A Space Invader motif stretches across his paunch. His jacket belongs to an army General's uniform: khaki, gold buttons, and rows of medals. From its pockets peep a magnifying glass, a wand, and an inch-thick manual. Above one shoulder of his superhero's cape points a sniper rifle, above the other a laser-cannon. His right hand is taped like a cage-fighter's while his left twirls a shuriken. He wears gangster sunglasses and an elvish cap.

> GATEKEEPER
> A contender, greetings. Let's see: what's your final score?

He gestures theatrically towards a giant totalizer, which furiously counts up and eventually stops, after a last-minute correction, at 26, 978, 452, 306, 143 (.9).

> PLAYER
> Point nine?

> GATEKEEPER
> You probably missed a collectible. Or collected a missable. 'S quite common.

> PLAYER
> But that's a lot, right? I mean, that's a long number.

> GATEKEEPER
> Not if we count very small things. We're fussy, you know, nothing gets past us. Once you round up, it's actually…

Counter ticks over to 3.

> PLAYER
> That's not so impressive.

> GATEKEEPER
> At least it's not minus.

Epilogue

> PLAYER
> So it's okay, three's… average?
>
> GATEKEEPER
> (grimaces and wavers one hand)
>
> PLAYER
> Well what does it mean, then? Is it out of ten?
>
> GATEKEEPER
> Just the other day someone got 158. Course, they still asked if they could go round again, to improve their score. Everybody tries that one. Like, do you remember there being Save points, on your birthday? I don't think so.
>
> PLAYER
> So you're supposed to get as high as possible? This is the number of bonuses you take into the final round, all I've got is three, and there's no way I can win from here?
>
> GATEKEEPER
> That's a new one. Actually no it isn't, I've heard them all before – I demand to see the referee, I couldn't complete such-and-such a mission because there was a glitch, where's my alternative ending – but it keeps me entertained. When game's over, game's over. That's your lot.

PLAYER holds up game controller and presses random buttons. Nothing happens.

> GATEKEEPER
> Er, this is a cut-scene. That won't work. So if you'd just be so kind, when you're quite ready, to step this way.

He attempts to usher PLAYER towards a small side-gate.

> PLAYER
> What's that? I'm not going through there.

> GATEKEEPER
> (puffing himself up)
> Now now, there's no need to get awkward.

> PLAYER
> But it's ridiculous: you can't sum a person's whole life up in a single number. Three?!

> GATEKEEPER
> Divine simplicity. You wouldn't believe the amount of work that goes into cleaning that counter.

> PLAYER
> I worked hard. I can't believe I didn't score more than that. I spent years, my whole life… There were always people telling you how you're supposed to live, but nothing that meant you could really know. How badly designed is that?

GATEKEEPER makes heard-it-all-before faces and merely holds the side-door open. PLAYER looks around but the main gates remain closed and all else is blank void.

> GATEKEEPER
> Don't be shy. You might like it.

PLAYER approaches side-gate and cautiously peers into the blackness within.

Epilogue

                    PLAYER
              (from threshold)
This may be a cut-scene, but I'm telling you, the
moment I go through this door, play will resume.

                    GATEKEEPER
You're the boss...

Eventually PLAYER exits, and the side-gate closes behind.

                    GATEKEEPER
And another happy customer. Roll up, roll up! Points
mean prizes! Do we have a winner?

                                        FADE to black.

Credits: Further reading

Arguments about the potential socio-political functions of play and the 'gamification' of real life are made by Pat Kane, *The Play Ethic: A Manifesto for a Different Way of Living* (Pan Macmillan, 2004); Alexander R. Galloway, *Gaming: Essays on Algorithmic Culture* (University of Minnesota Press, 2006); MacKenzie Wark, *Gamer Theory* (Harvard University Press, 2007); Christopher Monks, *The Ultimate Game Guide to Your Life: Or, the Video Game as Existential Metaphor* (TOW Books, 2008); Mary Flanagan, *Critical Play: Radical Game Design* (MIT Press, 2009); Markus Montola, Jaakko Stenros, and Annika Waern, *Pervasive Games, Theory and Design: Experiences on the Boundary Between Life and Play* (Morgan Kaufmann, 2009); Gabe Zichermann and Joselin Linder, *Game-based Marketing: Inspire Customer Loyalty Through Rewards, Challenges, and Contests* (John Wiley and Sons, 2010); and Jane McGonigal, *Reality is Broken: Why Games Make Us Better and How They Can Change the World* (Penguin, 2011). For a wider perspective on play, classic texts available in various editions are Johan Huizinga, *Homo Ludens: A Study of the Play Element in Culture* (1938), Roger Caillois, Man, Play, and Games (1958), Eric Berne, *Games People Play: The Psychology of Human Relationships* (1964), and Brian Sutton-Smith, *The Ambiguity of Play* (1997).

There's now a wide selection of introductory textbooks on Game Studies. Among the most readable are Steven Poole, *Trigger Happy: The Inner Life of Videogames* (Fourth Estate, 2000 and other editions) and

James Newman, *Videogames* (Routledge, 2004). More recent textbooks include Jason Rutter and Jo Bryce (eds.), *Understanding Digital Games* (Sage, 2006), Simon Egenfeldt-Nielsen, Jonas Heide Smith, and Susana Pajares Tosca, *Understanding Video Games: The Essential Introduction* (Routledge, 2008), and Frans Mäyrä, *An Introduction to Game Studies: Games and Culture* (Sage, 2008).

Adding up to over a thousand pages, Katie Salen and Eric Zimmerman's two volumes, *Rules of Play: Game Design Fundamentals* (MIT Press, 2004) and *The Game Design Reader: A Rules of Play Anthology* (MIT Press, 2006), offer a comprehensive and influential guide for both Game Design and Game Studies.

For debates about the educational value of games, your first port of call might be James Paul Gee's books, such as *What Video Games Have to Teach Us About Learning and Literacy* (Palgrave Macmillan, 2003).

For more strictly philosophical approaches to videogames, see Jon Cogburn and Mark Silcox, *Philosophy through Video Games* (Routledge, 2008) and Miguel Sicart, *The Ethics of Computer Games* (MIT Press, 2009). Open Court publishes some game-related titles, such as Luke Cuddy and John Nordlinger (eds.), *World of Warcraft and Philosophy: Wrath of the Philosopher King* (2009), in its Popular Culture and Philosophy series.

The *Game Studies* e-journal contains numerous academic papers covering a wide range of topics. Espen Aarseth's opening salvo for the first issue, 'Computer Game Studies Year One,' remains a key manifesto for the validity of this new discipline: http://www.gamestudies.org/0101/editorial.html. Or try *Eludamos: Journal for Computer Game Culture*, http://www.eludamos.org/ or *DiGRA* (Digital Games Research Association) *Digital Library*, http://www.digra.org/dl.

Online the range of writing about gaming is vast. Here's a brief, eclectic list of further recommendations relating, sometimes closely and sometimes loosely, to the individual missions. As with other online sources, some of the following may become unavailable over time. Googling the author and title of an item may help locate an alternative if the original has been deleted or moved (or provide faster access than typing in a long address).

p3. *Gameful*, http://www.gameful.org/.

p20. Jasper Juul, 'Games have rules,' *The Ludologist*, 1 December 2006, http://www.jesperjuul.net/ludologist/games-have-rules.

p24. Brice Morrison, 'The game design canvas: punishment and reward systems,' *The Game Prodigy*, February 2011, http://thegameprodigy.com/the-game-design-canvas-punishment-and-reward-systems/.

p28. John Harris, 'An intro to cellular automation,' *Gamasutra*, 4 May 2011, http://www.gamasutra.com/view/feature/6367/an_intro_to_cellular_automation.php.

p35. Ian Bogost and Cindy Poremba, 'Can games get real? a closer look at "documentary" digital games,' (2008), *Ian Bogost – Videogame Theory, Criticism, Design*, http://bogo.st/97.

p39. Michael Leader, 'Top five craziest uses of historical figures in video games,' *Den of Geek*, 17 July 2009, http://www.denofgeek.com/games/288359/top_five_craziest_uses_of_historical_figures_in_video_games.html.

p42. Andy Baio, 'Metagames: games about games,' *Waxy.org*, 1 February 2011, http://waxy.org/2011/02/metagames_games_about_games/.

p45. Elmer Tucker, 'The Orientalist perspective: cultural imperialism in gaming,' *Gameology*, 17 July 2006, http://www.gameology.org/alien_other/orientalist_perspective.

p48. 'Exquisite corpses!' *Jane McGonigal: Avant Game*, 2004, http://www.avantgame.com/exquisitecorpse.htm.

p51. http://audiogames.net/; Niklas Röber and Maic Masuch, 'Playing audio-only games: a compendium of interacting with virtual, auditory worlds,' *Proceedings of the Second DiGRA Games Conference*, 2005, http://www.x3t.net/documents/Roeber_2005_PAG.pdf.

p55. Henry Jenkins, 'Game design as narrative architecture,' *Henry Jenkins blog*, 2002, http://web.mit.edu/cms/People/henry3/games&narrative.html.

p65. Henry Jenkins, 'A few thoughts on media violence…' *Confessions of an Aca/Fan* archives, 25 April 2007, http://www.henryjenkins.

org/2007/04/a_few_thoughts_on_media_violen.html; Craig A. Anderson, 'FAQs on violent video games and other media violence,' *Craig A. Anderson website*, Centre for the Study of Violence, Department of Psychology, Iowa State University, 2009, http://www.psychology.iastate.edu/faculty/caa/Video_Game_FAQs.html.

p70. Reverend Dagger, 'The top 10 most blood-soaked video game weapons,' *SPIKE TV Official Website*, 17 November 2008, http://www.spike.com/articles/u3e7js/the-top-10-most-blood-soaked-video-game-weapons; Edgar Wright, 'Gun fetish (1993),' *Edgar Wright Here*, 4 April 2011, http://www.edgarwrighthere.com/2011/04/04/gun-fetish-1993/.

p73. Stephen Totilo, 'The Daddening of Video Games,' *Kotaku*, 9 February 2010, http://kotaku.com/5467695/the-daddening-of-video-games.

p79. Roger Travis, 'Living epic – the main quest,' *Living Epic: Video Games in the Ancient World*, 9 June 2008, http://livingepic.blogspot.com/2008/06/living-epic-main-quest-consolidation.html; Nick, 'The hero's journey and *Final Fantasy*: chapter 1,' *GameBlurb*, 28 March 2011, http://www.gameblurb.net/featured/the-heros-journey-and-final-fantasy-chapter-i/.

p83. always_black (Ian Shanahan), 'Bow nigger,' *always_black.com*, 22 September 2004, http://www.alwaysblack.com/blackbox/bownigger.html; Kieron Gillen, 'The New Games Journalism,' *Kieron Gillen's Workblog*, 2004, http://gillen.cream.org/wordpress_html/?page_id=3.

p85. John Walker, 'A death is for life, not just for quickload,' *Rock, Paper, Shotgun*, 12 May 2011, http://www.rockpapershotgun.com/2011/05/12/a-death-is-for-life-not-just-for-quickload.

p88. Joseph DeLappe, 'dead-in-iraq,' *Joseph DeLappe website*, 2009, http://www.unr.edu/art/delappe/gaming/dead_in_iraq/dead_in_iraq%20jpegs.html.

p91. Susan J. Robertson, Jane Leonard, and Alex J. Chamberlain, 'PlayStation purpura,' *Australasian Journal of Dermatology* 51: 3 (2010), http://onlinelibrary.wiley.com/doi/10.1111/j.1440-0960.2010.00652.x/pdf.

p97. Edmond Chang, 'Close playing: a meditation on teaching (with) video games,' *EDagogy*, 11 November 2010, http://staff.washington.edu/changed/2010/11/close-playing-a-meditation/.

p102. Richard Bartle, 'Bartle Test of Player Psychology,' *gamerDNA.com*, http://www.gamerdna.com/quizzes/bartle-test-of-gamer-psychology; G. Christopher Klug and Jesse Schell, 'Why People Play Games: An Industry Perspective,' summary available at http://playertypes.org/research/?q=node/82.

p105. *GameLog*, http://www.gamelog.cl/.

p109. Anthony Burch, 'The end, my friend: the difficulty in creating an awesome game ending,' *Destructoid*, 11 June 2007, http://www.destructoid.com/the-end-my-friend-the-difficulty-in-creating-an-awesome-ending-to-a-videogame-32662.phtml.

p117. RoboCup objective, 2010, http://www.robocup.org/about-robocup/objective/.

p120. Ian Bogost, 'Persuasive games: video game Zen,' *Gamasutra*, 29 November 2007, http://www.gamasutra.com/view/feature/2585/persuasive_games_video_game_zen.php.

p123. Robbie Cooper, Immersion video, *Robbie Cooper website*, 2008, http://www.robbiecooper.org/ then click Simulations, Immersion, Photos, Play video.

p126. Cathal Horan, 'Bored with time?' *Philosophy Now 65*, January/February 2008, http://www.philosophynow.org/issue65/Bored_With_Time.

p129. Gary Wolf, 'Know thyself: tracking every facet of life, from sleep to mood to pain, 24/7/365,' *Wired*, 22 June 2009, http://www.wired.com/medtech/health/magazine/17-07/lbnp_knowthyself.

p132. Drew Davidson, 'Snackable Games,' *Tap Repeatedly*, 10 January 2011, http://tap-repeatedly.com/2011/01/10/celebrity-guest-editorial-drew-davidson-part-2/; Lajos (Lajos Ishibashi Brons), 'A FAQ for the slow games movement,' *BoardGameGeek*, 7 August 2007, http://www.boardgamegeek.com/geeklist/23629/a-faq-for-the-slow-games-movement.

p139. David Thomas, José P. Zagal, Margaret Robertson, Ian Bogost, and William Huber, 'You played that? Game studies meets game criticism,' *Digital Games Research Association (DiGRA) Digital Library*, 2009, http://www.digra.org/dl/db/09287.17255.pdf.

p144. David Griner, 'To hell and back: EA's guerilla marketing campaign for "Dante's Inferno,"' *AdFreak.com*, 24 February 2010, http://adweek.blogs.com/adfreak/electronic-arts-marketing-of-dantes-inferno.html; Tim Buckley, 'Marketing hell,' *Ctrl+Alt+Del* webcomic, 11 September 2009, http://www.cad-comic.com/cad/20090911.

p148. Tom Boellstorff, 'A ludicrous discipline? Ethnography and game studies,' *Games and Culture* 1: 1 (2006), http://www.anthro.uci.edu/faculty_bios/boellstorff/Boellstorff-Games.pdf.

p150. Robert Coles, 'Doing documentary work,' *The Washington Post*, 1997, http://www.washingtonpost.com/wp-srv/style/longterm/books/chap1/doingdocumentarywork.htm.

p154. *Stick Page*, http://www.stickpage.com/; Eric Lewallen, 'A history of the stick figure,' video talk, *words are pictures too*, February 2008, http://wordsarepicturestoo.wordpress.com/2008/02/07/a-history-of-the-stick-figure/.

p157. Tim Hunkin, 'Mobility masterclass,' *Tim Hunkin home page*, 2005, http://www.timhunkin.com/a113_Mobility_Masterclass.htm; Iain Sharp, 'Lunar lander,' *www.lushprojects.com*, 2009, http://www.lushprojects.com/lunarlander/.

p163. Ryan Scott, 'My dad, the gamer,' *GameSpy*, 6 May 2011, http://www.gamespy.com/articles/116/1166461p1.html.

p173. *Gamers' Voice*, http://gamersvoice.org.uk/.

p175. James Paul Gee, 'Good video games and good learning,' Phi Kappa Phi Forum Summer 2005, http://jamespaulgee.com/sites/default/files/pub/GoodVideoGamesLearning.pdf; New Learning Institute, 'Katie Salen,' *Vimeo*, 11 October 2010, http://vimeo.com/15732859.

p178. Jennifer Gabrys, 'five: media in the dump,' chapter 5 of *Digital Rubbish: A Natural History of Electronics*, Digital Culture Books, University of Michigan Press, 2011, http://www.digitalculture.org/books/digital-rubbish, chapter available at http://hdl.handle.net/2027/spo.9380304.0001.001.

About the author

Andrew Cutting is a Senior Lecturer in the Faculty of Social Sciences and Humanities at London Metropolitan University, where he teaches Game Studies, English Literature, and Professional Writing. He is also the author of *Death in Henry James*.